First World War
and Army of Occupation
War Diary
France, Belgium and Germany

40 DIVISION
121 Infantry Brigade,
Brigade Machine Gun Company
15 June 1916 - 28 February 1918

WO95/2616/3

The Naval & Military Press Ltd
www.nmarchive.com
Published in association with The National Archives

Published by

The Naval & Military Press Ltd

Unit 10 Ridgewood Industrial Park,

Uckfield, East Sussex,

TN22 5QE England

Tel: +44 (0) 1825 749494

www.naval-military-press.com

www.nmarchive.com

This diary has been reprinted in facsimile from the original. Any imperfections are inevitably reproduced and the quality may fall short of modern type and cartographic standards.

© Crown Copyright
Images reproduced by permission of The National Archives, London, England, 2015.

Contents

Document type	Place/Title	Date From	Date To
Heading	WO95/2616/3		
Heading	40th Division 121st Infy Bde 121st Machine Gun Coy. Jun 1916-Feb 1918		
Heading	War Diary Of No 121 Machine Gun Coy Machine Gun Corps From 15th June 1916 To 30th June 1916 (Volume I)		
War Diary	Grantham	15/06/1916	15/06/1916
War Diary	Southampton	16/06/1916	16/06/1916
War Diary	Le Havre	17/06/1916	18/06/1916
War Diary	Bruay	19/06/1916	19/06/1916
War Diary	Bois D'Olhain	20/06/1916	20/06/1916
War Diary	Bois D'Olhain	21/06/1916	30/06/1916
Miscellaneous	Appendix No 1	18/06/1916	18/06/1916
Miscellaneous	Appendix No 2	27/06/1916	27/06/1916
Miscellaneous	121st M.G. Com	01/07/1916	01/07/1916
Heading	War Diary of No 121 Bde M.G. Coy Machine Gun Corps. From 1st July 1916 To 31st July 1916 Volume 2		
War Diary	Bois. D'Olhain	01/07/1916	02/07/1916
War Diary	Les Brebis	03/07/1916	31/07/1916
Heading	War Diary of No 121 Machine Gun Company Machine Gun Corps From 1st August 1916 to August 1916 Volume 3		
War Diary	Les Brebis	01/08/1916	06/08/1916
War Diary	Houchin	07/08/1916	09/08/1916
War Diary	Les Brebis	10/08/1916	31/08/1916
Miscellaneous	O.C. 121 Machine Gun Corps app I	08/08/1916	08/08/1916
Miscellaneous	Operation of Work	08/08/1916	08/08/1916
Miscellaneous	Programme of Work	09/08/1916	09/08/1916
Miscellaneous	Programme of Work	10/08/1916	10/08/1916
Heading	War Diary of 121st Machine Gun Company Machine Gun Corps From 1st Sept 1916 To 30th Sept 1916 Volume 3		
War Diary	Les Brebis	01/09/1916	30/09/1916
Heading	War Diary of 121 Machine Gun Coy Machine Gun Corps. 1st October 1916 to 31st October 1916 Vol 5		
War Diary	Les Brebis	01/10/1916	28/10/1916
War Diary	Bruay	29/10/1916	29/10/1916
War Diary	Le Tirlet	30/10/1916	31/10/1916
Heading	War Diary of 121 Machine Gun Company from 1st November 1916 to 1st December 1916 Volume 6		
War Diary	Le Tirlet	01/11/1916	01/11/1916
War Diary	Houvigneul	02/11/1916	03/11/1916
War Diary	Barly	04/11/1916	04/11/1916
War Diary	Berneuil	05/11/1916	14/11/1916
War Diary	Remaisnil	15/11/1916	16/11/1916
War Diary	Neuvillette	17/11/1916	17/11/1916
War Diary	Sus-St-Leger.	18/11/1916	21/11/1916
War Diary	Authieule	22/11/1916	22/11/1916
War Diary	Halloy	23/11/1916	23/11/1916
War Diary	Pont Remy	24/11/1916	25/11/1916

War Diary	Brucamps	26/11/1916	30/11/1916
Miscellaneous	Headquarters 40th Division.	30/10/1916	30/10/1916
Miscellaneous	Routine Orders By Major-General H.G. Ruggles-Brise C.B. M.V.O. Commanding 40th Division.	01/11/1916	01/11/1916
Miscellaneous	(C) No 45283 Private Owen Thristan 121st Machine Gun Company		
Miscellaneous	121 Machine Gun Company	27/11/1916	27/11/1916
Miscellaneous	To Hqrs 121 Inf Bde.	02/01/1917	02/01/1917
Heading	War Diary of 121 Machine Gun Coy. From 1 December 1916 to 31st December 1916 Volume 6		
War Diary	Brucamp	01/12/1916	10/12/1916
War Diary	Sailley-Laurette	11/12/1916	26/12/1916
War Diary	Camp. 17. (Suzanne)	27/12/1916	31/12/1916
Miscellaneous	121 Machine Gun Company	16/12/1916	16/12/1916
Miscellaneous	121 Machine Gun Company	09/12/1916	09/12/1916
Miscellaneous	Headquarters No 333 G 22nd Dec 1916 121st Infantry Bde.	22/12/1916	22/12/1916
Heading	War Diary of 121 Machine Gun Company Machine Gun Corps. from 1st January 1917 to 31st January 1917 Volume 8		
War Diary	Bouchavesnes	01/01/1917	08/01/1917
War Diary	Suzanne	09/01/1917	12/01/1917
War Diary	Rancourt	13/01/1917	22/01/1917
War Diary	Suzanne	23/01/1917	24/01/1917
War Diary	Chipilly	25/01/1917	31/01/1917
Heading	War Diary of 121 Machine Gun Company from 1st February 1917 To 28th February 1917 Volume 8		
War Diary	Camp 12 Chipilly	01/02/1917	10/02/1917
War Diary	Camp III Bray	11/02/1917	19/02/1917
War Diary	Le Forest	20/02/1917	21/02/1917
War Diary	Rancourt	22/02/1917	28/02/1917
Heading	War Diary of 121 Machine Gun Coy Machine Gun Corps from 1st March 1917 to 31st March 1917 Volume 9		
War Diary	Rancourt	01/03/1917	07/03/1917
War Diary	Suzanne	08/03/1917	13/03/1917
War Diary	Curlu	14/03/1917	15/03/1917
War Diary	Clery	16/03/1917	18/03/1917
War Diary	Perronne	19/03/1917	19/03/1917
War Diary	Mt St Quentin	20/03/1917	20/03/1917
War Diary	Mont-St-Quentin	21/03/1917	31/03/1917
Miscellaneous	To Hqrs 121st Inf Brigade	01/05/1917	01/05/1917
Heading	War Diary of 121 Machine Gun Company Machine Gun Corps. from 1st April 1917 to 30th April 1917 Volume 10		
War Diary	Mount-St-Quentin	01/04/1917	05/04/1917
War Diary	Equancourt	06/04/1917	07/04/1917
War Diary	Fins	08/04/1917	17/04/1917
War Diary	Etricourt	18/04/1917	23/04/1917
War Diary	Fins	24/04/1917	27/04/1917
War Diary	Dessart Wood (W. 1b. 7.0)	28/04/1917	30/04/1917
Miscellaneous	To Headquarters 121 Infy Brigade	01/06/1917	01/06/1917
Heading	War Diary of 121 Machine Gun Coy Machine Gun Corps from 1st May 1917 to 31st May 1917 Volume No 11		
War Diary	Dessart Wood	01/05/1917	12/05/1917

Type	Description	Start	End
War Diary	Heudecourt	13/05/1917	13/05/1917
War Diary	Villers Guislians	14/05/1917	22/05/1917
War Diary	Dessart Wood	23/05/1917	31/05/1917
Miscellaneous	Summary. Casualties	31/05/1917	31/05/1917
Miscellaneous	Operation Order By Major P Mathisen. O.C. 121 Machine Gun Company	05/05/1917	05/05/1917
Heading	Report on Operations on the night of 5th 6th May 1917 at LA Vacquerie 0		
Miscellaneous	Map. Refer T.S. 54/1/10000		
Miscellaneous	Report on Operations at La Vacquerie on 5th 6th May 1917 121 Machine Gun Company	09/05/1917	09/05/1917
Miscellaneous	Indirect Overhead Fire	05/05/1917	05/05/1917
Operation(al) Order(s)	121st. Infantry Brigade Order No 93	05/05/1917	05/05/1917
Miscellaneous	Machine Gun Barrage	05/05/1917	05/05/1917
Map			
Heading	121 Machine Gun Company War Diary Volume 12 June 1917		
War Diary	Dessart Wood	01/06/1917	10/06/1917
War Diary	Gonnelieu	10/06/1917	26/06/1917
War Diary	Dessart Valley	26/06/1917	30/06/1917
Map	Brigade Boundary		
Miscellaneous	Reinforcements	13/06/1917	13/06/1917
Miscellaneous	To Hospital		
Heading	War Diary of 121 Coy Machine Gun Corps from 1st July 1917 to 31st July 1917 Volume 13		
War Diary	Villers-Guislain	01/07/1917	31/07/1917
Miscellaneous	Copy of Daily Report Appendix I	25/07/1917	25/07/1917
Miscellaneous	For Month ending 31st July 1917	31/07/1917	31/07/1917
Heading	War Diary of 121st Machine Gun Corps from 1st August 1917 to 31st August 1917 Volume 14		
War Diary	Gonnelieu Viller Guislain	01/08/1917	31/08/1917
Miscellaneous	Killed Wounded Admitted to Hospital	31/08/1917	31/08/1917
Heading	War Diary of 121st Company Machine Gun Corps from 1st September 1917 to 30th September 1917 Volume 15		
War Diary	Gonnelieu Villers Guislain	01/09/1917	17/09/1917
Heading	Report on Operations on the night of 5th 6th May 1917 at La Vacquerie		
War Diary	Gonnelieu & Villers Guislain	18/09/1917	30/09/1917
Miscellaneous	Operation Orders By Major. P. Mathisen Commanding 121st Company Machine Gun Corps.	22/09/1917	22/09/1917
Map	Barrage Map Appendix I		
Miscellaneous	Casualties Wounded Admitted to hospital	30/09/1917	30/09/1917
Heading	War Diary of 121st Company Machine Gun Corps from 1st October 1917 to 31st October 1917 Volume 16		
War Diary	Heudicourt	01/10/1917	10/10/1917
War Diary	Peronne	11/10/1917	12/10/1917
War Diary	La Herliere	13/10/1917	29/10/1917
War Diary	Sombrin	30/10/1917	31/10/1917
Heading	War Diary of 121st Machine Gun Corps from 1st November 1917 to 30 November 1917 Volume 17		
War Diary	Sombrin	01/11/1917	16/11/1917
War Diary	La Hurliere	17/11/1917	18/11/1917
War Diary	Achiet-Le-Petit	19/11/1917	19/11/1917
War Diary	Rocquigny	20/11/1917	21/11/1917
War Diary	Beaumetz	22/11/1917	22/11/1917
War Diary	Gohincourt	23/11/1917	26/11/1917

War Diary	Bertincourt	27/11/1917	30/11/1917
Heading	War Diary of 121st Company Machine Gun Corps from 1st December 1917 to 31st December 1917 Volume 18		
War Diary	Bellacourt	01/12/1917	01/12/1917
War Diary	Ervillers	02/12/1917	02/12/1917
War Diary	Croisilles Sector.	03/12/1917	10/12/1917
War Diary	Ervillers	11/12/1917	11/12/1917
War Diary	Croisilles	12/12/1917	24/12/1917
War Diary	Muyenne Ville	25/12/1917	26/12/1917
War Diary	Bullecourt	27/12/1917	31/12/1917
Heading	War Diary of 121st Company Machine Gun Corps from 1st January 1918 to 31st January 1918 Volume 19		
War Diary	Bullecourt	01/01/1918	07/01/1918
War Diary	Ervillers	08/01/1918	15/01/1918
War Diary	Bullecourt	16/01/1918	31/01/1918
Heading	War Diary of "C" Coy 40th Div. M.G. Battalion. From 1st February 1918 To 28th February 1918 Volume 20		
War Diary	Bullecourt	01/02/1918	12/02/1918
War Diary	Moyenneville	13/02/1918	14/02/1918
War Diary	No 4 Camp Hendecourt	15/02/1918	18/02/1918
War Diary	Durham Camp Boisleux Au Mont	19/02/1918	26/02/1918
War Diary	Durrow Camp Mory	27/02/1918	28/02/1918

WO95/26192/3

40TH DIVISION
121ST INFY BDE

121ST MACHINE GUN COY.

JUN 1916 - FEB 1918

40TH DIVISION
121ST INFY BDE

Original copy

Confidential

"War Diary"
of
No 121 Machine Gun Coy
Machine Gun Corps

from 15th June 1916 to 30th June 1916

1 (Volume I)

Feb '18

121 M G Coy
Army Form C. 2118.

Vol I

WAR DIARY
or
INTELLIGENCE SUMMARY
(Erase heading not required.)

Instructions regarding War Diaries and Intelligence Summaries are contained in F. S. Regs., Part II. and the Staff Manual respectively. Title Pages will be prepared in manuscript.

Place	Date	Hour	Summary of Events and Information	Remarks and references to Appendices
Grantham	15/6/16		The 121st Machine Gun Company was formed at Grantham on the 14th March 1916 and was mobilized on the 15th June 1916 for service overseas. On the night of the 15th June 1916 we entrained at Grantham. Officers were as follows:— Capt. P. Mathisen 2/Lt. J. M. Weaver Lt. B. R. Thomas 2/Lt. E. L. Sartin " H. A. Cutler " G. L. Rowe " R. L. Stockley " A. P. Male " A. M. R. Bain " S. A. Wann.	

Army Form C. 2118.

WAR DIARY
or
INTELLIGENCE SUMMARY
(Erase heading not required.)

Instructions regarding War Diaries and Intelligence Summaries are contained in F.S. Regs., Part II. and the Staff Manual respectively. Title Pages will be prepared in manuscript.

Place	Date	Hour	Summary of Events and Information	Remarks and references to Appendices
Southampton SOUTHAMPTON	16/6/16		The 131st Machine Gun Coy. arrived at Southampton about 11 a.m. and entrained at once. The Company was split into two parties, of 7 Officers and 100 O.R. who entrained on board H.M.T. "Caesarea", and 3 Officers and 43 O.R. with transport, which entrained on H.M.T. "BELLEROPHON" at 6.30 p.m., leaving SOUTHAMPTON at 10 p.m.	
LE HAVRE	17/6/16		The "CAESAREA" arrived at LE HAVRE about 11 a.m. after a very rough passage. We were sent to No.1 Rest Camp where we remained the night.	See App. I
"	18/6/16		We left No.1 Rest Camp at 4.30 p.m. and proceeded to the Gare MARITIME to entrain, leaving LE HAVRE at 9.30 p.m. There was one casualty.	
BRUAY	19/6/16		We arrived here about 7.30 p.m. (about 9 hours late) and went into billets at FOSSE 9, BARLIN. Map reference Sheet 36b S.E. scale 20000 Q.14.B.14.	
BOIS D'OLHAIN	20/6/16		On this date 16 N.C.O.'s and 48 O.R. were attached to the various battalions in the Brigade for instruction in Vickers	

Army Form C. 2118.

WAR DIARY
or
INTELLIGENCE SUMMARY

(Erase heading not required.)

Instructions regarding War Diaries and Intelligence Summaries are contained in F. S. Regs., Part II. and the Staff Manual respectively. Title Pages will be prepared in manuscript.

Place	Date	Hour	Summary of Events and Information	Remarks and references to Appendices
B615 D'ELHAIN	21/6/16		The Company was inspected at BRUAY by General Sir Charles Munro, G.O.C. 10th Army (Corps). One N.C.O. was detailed for a Course of Anti-Gas Measures at AIRE.	
"	22/6/16		Proceeded to H.Q. 1st Inf. Bde, MINE BUILDINGS, LES BREBIS, to arrange for the Company to receive a course of Instruction in Trench Work; this course to last from 24.6.16. to 8.7.16. in the CALONNE Sector. Trench Stores ('T' Steel Helmets, &c) were drawn. Coy. Training (Capt. R.C. Ross)	
"	23/6/16		The first Half-Company (3 Nos 1 & 2 Secs. left billets at 1.30 p.m. & proceeded to LES BREBIS, for 4 days instruction in trenches. The remainder of the Coy were left in charge of 2/Lt Weever 2nd in Command).	
"	24/6/16		The Hand (Company) training & instruction was carried on by Nos 3 & 4 Secs, Capt. P. Mathiesen, Lt. B.R.S. Thomas, 2/Lt A.M.R. Rain, 2/Lt B.L. Sahn, 2/Lt G.L. Rose, & SS P.R. remained in the trenches at LES BREBIS.	
"	25/6/16			
"	26/6/16		Company Training was carried on by Nos 3 & 4 Secs, and instruction at LES BREBIS, by Nos 1 & 2 Secs.	
"	27/6/16		Company Training was carried out. Nos 1 & 2 Secs at the instruction; casualties 3 (R. wounded); A/Cpl Daly (at duty) instruction at LES BREBIS (casualties, 3 (R. wounded); A/Cpl Daly (at duty); Pte Window E. (in Hospital) + PR Treanor (at duty)	Appendix No 2.
"	28/6/16		2nd Half Company relieved first half (oy) at 5.30 p.m. No 2 & 3 Sections	

Army Form C. 2118.

WAR DIARY
or
INTELLIGENCE SUMMARY

(Erase heading not required.)

Place	Date	Hour	Summary of Events and Information	Remarks and references to Appendices
BOIS D'OLHAIN	28/8/16		Sent into the Trenches at CALONNE Sector and No 1 and 2 Sections returning to Billets at BOIS D'OLHAIN.	
	29/8/16		The usual Company Training was carried on; No 3 & 4 Secs. still in Trenches with 1st. Inf. Bgd at LES BREBIS. (CALONNE Sector.	
"	30/8/16		The usual Company Training was carried on; & No 3 & 4 Secs ten are still in the Trenches at LES BREBIS receiving instruction in Trench Work, Warfare.	

P Mathison Capt.
O.C. 121 M.G. Coy.
M.G. Corps.

Appendix No 1.

1st Casualty was Sgt. P. Keogh. of No 1 Section who was left behind at the "Casino Hospital" with a Blood Poisoned Hand & we were informed that one finger would be amputated.

"HAVRE"
18-6-16.

P Mathisen Capt
O.C. 121 M.G. Coy.

Appendix No 2.

On the night & morning of the 26th-27th/6-16 during a rather heavy Trench Mortar & Shell bombardment of the CALLONNE SECTOR of Trench one of the covered Machine Gun Emplacements was blown in & Pvt. C. Wisdom was seriously wounded in the legs, arms & back by splinters of Shell & Bricks.

L.Cpl. Daly & Pvt Treanor were also injured, being very badly crushed & bruised by falling walls, bricks etc. Pvt Wisdom was taken to the Hospital but L.Cpl Daly & Pvt Treanor both after a short rest resumed their duties.

P. Mathisen. Capt.
O.C. 121 M.G. Coy.

"LES BREBIS."
27-6-16.

121st M.G. Coy

Diary returned herewith.

It is all right. You'll hardly be able to go into such detail about casualties in appendices when things begin to hum.

It should be sent off today in accordance with F.S.R. II

A.M. Thomson Capt.
B.M. 121 Bde

1/7/16

Original (copy)

40

121. M G C
Vol 2

Confidential.

War Diary.
of
No 121 Bde M.G. Coy.
Machine Gun Corps.

From 1st July 1916. to 31st July 1916.

Volume 2

Army Form C. 2118.

WAR DIARY
or
INTELLIGENCE SUMMARY
(Erase heading not required.)

Instructions regarding War Diaries and Intelligence Summaries are contained in F.S. Regs., Part II. and the Staff Manual respectively. Title Pages will be prepared in manuscript.

Place	Date	Hour	Summary of Events and Information	Remarks and references to Appendices
BOIS d'OHLAIN	1-7-16		The half Coy consisting of No 1 & 2 Sections carried on with the usual M.G. work & training also the Instructional Class. The other half Coy consisting of No 3 & 4 Section is still in the CALLONNE SECTOR of Trenches undergoing 4 days instruction in Trench work & Warfare. 2nd Lt Q.L. Shockley & 4 O.R's were relieved from the trenches & returned to Camp in order to leave BARLIN SEN on the 2nd July & proceed to CAMIERE for a 20 days Machine Gun Course commencing 3-7-16.	
	2-7-16		Orders were received from 121st Infantry Bde that the O.C. & 7 other officers would proceed to LES BREBIS to reconnoitre the MAROC SECTOR of Trenches, occupied by the 2nd Infantry Bde, with a view to taking over this section later in the day.	
LES BREBIS	3-7-16		The 121 M.G. Coy received orders to leave BOIS d'OHLAIN at 1.30 p.m. & proceed to LES BREBIS. The 121 M.G. Coy arrived at 6 p.m. & relieved the 2nd M.G. Coy taking over the MAROC SECTOR the relief being completed at 2 a.m. There were 3 officers, 73 other ranks with 15 guns placed in this sector	
	4-7-16		Conditions normal. Enemy very quiet. Our Artillery was very active between the hours of 12 - 1.30 a.m. 3-4th July. There are 6 officers, 62 O.R's of 121 M.G. Coy 62 O.R. attached to the Coy in Billets at LES BREBIS. The usual Instructional work is going on with the attached men. Orders were received for an organised Strafe & 6 guns were laid on GAPS in wire, CROSS RDS BACK BILLETS, DUMPS & COMMUNICATION TRENCHES, firing to be carried out irregular at intervals commencing at 11 p.m. 5th July 1916 until 4 a.m. 6th July 1916.	
	5-7-16		Our artillery was again very active from 12 MIDNIGHT to 1.30 a.m. 4 - 5 July.	

2449 Wt. W14957/M90 750,000 1/16 J.B.C. & A. Forms/C.2118/12.

WAR DIARY
or
INTELLIGENCE SUMMARY

(Erase heading not required.)

Army Form C. 2118.

Place	Date	Hour	Summary of Events and Information	Remarks and references to Appendices
LES BREBIS	5/7/16		Firing has been carried on as per orders. the guns firing very well but RESULTS UNKNOWN. Weather is very changeable, sudden thunderstorms with heavy rains. 1st CORPS HEAVY ARTILLERY opened fire from 8 p.m to 10 p.m 5/7-16 searching XI Corps counter Roads &c at BOIS de QUATORZE with a view to assisting XI Corps counter battery. 2 Ptes arrived from BETHUNE to replace casualties No. 32814 Pte WOODAGE. H. No. 35404 Pte DAVIS.A.	
	6-7-16		1st CORPS Heavy Artillery was active during the forenoon & No.1 Armoured train co-operated. During the hours of 1 a.m & 3 p.m bof on guns were firing at communication trenches, Back Billets, Dugouts etc. the enemy retaliated with shelling & trench Mortars but very little damage was reported. The attached men are still ungoing instruction in Billets.	
	7/7/16		Firing was carried out by 6 guns at the following bombs (i.e. Back Billets, Dugouts etc.) M.10.C.2.5.5, M.10.B.1.1, M.10.A.8.1, M.10.A.7.9, M.10.A.7.7, M.10.A.7.4, M.10.A.9.8 to M.10.B.5.5, M.11.C. M.5.C.4.5 to M.5.C.9.2, M.11.B+D 1st troops Heavy Artillery opened fire on Billets, Houses etc at 12 noon. 3.30 p.m + 10 p.m. Enemy was very quiet. The attached men were inspected in Machine Gun work Transport, Signalling &c Mules were inspected. 3 extra men reported for duty from 20th Middlesex + 3 men from 21st Middlesex Regt. Received S.O.S. more at 4.45.a.m. cancelled at 4.45.a.m.	
	8-4-16		Firing was carried on until 10.30 p.m when working parties went out. French Mortar Battery very active on enemy front line. Enemy retaliated with H.E. H.Q + 5.9 shells. Aeroplanes searching out front line & one Machine Gun reported about communication trenches without visible 3 hun reported from the 12th Suffolks + 3 men from the 13th yorks to be permanently attached.	
	9/7/16		Firing was carried on at various selected points. Our Artillery was again	

Army Form C. 2118.

WAR DIARY
or
INTELLIGENCE SUMMARY
(Erase heading not required.)

Instructions regarding War Diaries and Intelligence Summaries are contained in F. S. Regs., Part II. and the Staff Manual respectively. Title Pages will be prepared in manuscript.

Place	Date	Hour	Summary of Events and Information	Remarks and references to Appendices
LES BREBIS	9-7-16		very active. Enemy snipers were very active & it is reported that there had been one spotted in the Double Grassier. At about 8 p.m. 16 of our aeroplanes crossed over the enemy lines at about 7,000 ft under a very heavy anything fire which was not effective.	
	10-7-16		Firing was carried on at selected points & good observation was obtained. The enemy replied with one gun but no damage was done unfortunately we could not engage this gun as several working parties were out. Enemy sniper was located at M.4.d.8.4. (Double Grassier) Map of 36°S.W. Several sniper posts have been located at this point. Transport, Mule & Harness Inspection.	
	11-7-16		Our artillery did great amount of damage to enemy front line. Trench Mortars & Bombing parties of the enemy were very active on South Grassier M.9.C.9.3 & M.10.C.5.B. Nothing particular responsible for our not engaging enemy gun firing from M.4.d.1.6 as we have noticed strict orders not to fire without particular orders. About 11 p.m. enemy search lights were very active at 11.30 p.m one of our aeroplanes came from over the enemy lines showing 3 white lights & travelling very fast.	
	12-7-16		The Boy was relieved this morning by 12D Bat. M.G. Coy at 4 a.m. & we have been placed in Reserve (Divisional). There are 2 Guns posted in the Reserve Line at Z POINT. Map Ref. sheet 36°S.W 20000. M.14.8.9.4. The remainder of the Guns are track at Billets. The first lot of attached men are sufficiently trained to go into trenches for a turn of Infantry duty. Only through to add to qualify them as Machine Gunners.	

2449 Wt. W14957/M90 750,000 1/16 J.B.C. & A. Forms/C2118/12.

Army Form C. 2118.

WAR DIARY
or
INTELLIGENCE SUMMARY
(Erase heading not required.)

Instructions regarding War Diaries and Intelligence Summaries are contained in F. S. Regs., Part II. and the Staff Manual respectively. Title Pages will be prepared in manuscript.

Place	Date	Hour	Summary of Events and Information	Remarks and references to Appendices
LES BREBIS	13-7-16		The M.G. Corps men who have been relieved have received clean clothing the Inspection was held & then they had a Route march. The attached men are carrying on with Inspection of night and morning. There enemy has been very quiet. Transport, Standards, Pack Inspection. Officers remounted the Reserve Line etc. Weather very fine, cool & dry.	
	14-7-16		The attached men are still carrying on with Instructional work. Guns have been overhauled, Elevating & Traversing dials fitted. The gun teams at "Z. POINT" are having a very quiet time, the Emplacements & Dugouts etc are in splendid condition. A miniature Range has been constructed & the attached men commence firing at 2 p.m. 15- July 1916. Weather remains fine.	
	15-7-16		All the Coy was on Instructional Work. Attached men were firing on miniature Range at 2 p.m. Results Excellent. Weather fine. Enemy very quiet.	
	16-7-16		The Coy was Bathing from 9 a.m. until 11.30 a.m. There were 4 Officers sent to me at 9 a.m. from the 20th & 21st Middlesex Regt/3 Yorks Regt & 12th Suffolks Regt for a Vickers Machine Gun Course. Attached men were on miniature Range at 2 p.m. Results Excellent. Orders were received dismissed that this Coy would relieve No 120 M. G. Coy in Manor Scots at 4 a.m. 19-7-16 with 15 Vickers Guns. The Guns will be withdrawn from "Z POINT" after relief has been completed, one to go into the Manor Shigrolls & the other one to the Billets for Instructional Purposes. Enemy very quiet. Weather unsettled raining from 11 a.m. during whole afternoon	

2449 Wt. W14957/Mg0 750,000 1/16 J.B.C. & A. Forms/C.2118/12.

Army Form C. 2118.

WAR DIARY
or
INTELLIGENCE SUMMARY
(Erase heading not required.)

Instructions regarding War Diaries and Intelligence Summaries are contained in F.S. Regs., Part II. and the Staff Manual respectively. Title Pages will be prepared in manuscript.

Place	Date	Hour	Summary of Events and Information	Remarks and references to Appendices
LES BREBIS	17-7-16		At 3 a.m. the Coy paraded & returned. No. 120 M.G. Coy. in MAROC Sector. The Coy was complimented by 8.30 a.m. There is a lot of work to be done on the trenches & several new dugouts & emplacements to be constructed.	
	18-7-16		Everything has been fairly quiet & although our artillery has been very active on enemy wire, the enemy has not retaliated beyond the usual Stokes Mortar H.E. & S.G. on front & support lines. Training is still going on & the attached guns have been firing on the 30 yds range with very good result. Weather fine.	
	19-7-16		The weather has been tropical. Our Artillery is still very active cutting wire. The Raid the 20th Middlesex were making on German Lines at M.H.Q 64/5½ to M.10.A.6.4 was postponed owing to wire not being sufficiently cut. The usual trench Mortar activity on front lines. Coy reached its first Bay in France. The largest a/c number having been recorded this morning.	
	20-7-16		The enemy is very quiet. Our Artillery is still very active. Enemy wire about 9/b is demolished. about 20 strapped stiles with LES BREBIS. No damage was done. Raiding parties from 20th Middlesex Regt & Patrol's from the 13th Yorkshire Regt. went over the parapet under cover of a heavy barrage of our Artillery at 10.30 p.m. The last party returning at 11.35 p.m. at 11.35 p.m. our front line Machine Guns opened the strong fire, the enemy's parapet, our fire must have been very effective as the enemy could be out manning their fire bays & this heard rather a splendid target reports from various parts of our line show that many of the enemy were accounted for. Weather Good.	
	21-7-16		Today Orders were received to withdraw 6 guns from the Right Subsection & to hand over that portion of Maroc Section to the 120 M.G. Coy. Instructions were also received that this Coy had to take over the LOOS Sector, with a Machine ENGLISH ALLEY, from the 48th M.G. Coy 16th Division.	

2449 Wt. W14957/M90 750,000 1/16 J.B.C. & A. Forms/C.2118/12.

WAR DIARY or INTELLIGENCE SUMMARY

Army Form C. 2118.

Place	Date	Hour	Summary of Events and Information	Remarks and references to Appendices
LES BREBIS	21-7-16		On the 22nd July 1916. The O.C. Coy proceeded to MASINGARBE + arranged for the relief of No 48 M.G Coy at 2 P.M. 22nd inst. 2/Lt G. Rowe reported to Coy Headqrs having withdrawn 6 guns from Right section of MAROC everything handed over correct. Casualties Nil. At 10.30 p.m. 2/Lt ROWE reports having disposed a working party repairing enemy wire as he was leaving the trench (front line) The enemy shelled LES BREBIS at 10 p.m with shrapnel. Damage Nil.	
	22-7-16		The enemy fairly quiet in Maroc sector except for usual shelling + trench Mortars on front & support lines. At 2 p.m we used 1st & 8th M.G Coy guns at MASINGARBE & took over Reserve line of trenches in LOOS sector putting in 1 gun S. Francis fire was carried out by our LEFT gun (R8 LOOS Section) to assist the Hy Bde in a raid on enemy trenches at H.31.B.2.5. The usual Indirect fire was carried on in MAROC LEFT sector on Dumps, Cross Rds, + Back Billets etc. the enemy retaliated for 2 hours with H.2's on QUEEN St + CARFAX Rd. Damage Nil. Casualties Nil. Weather fine. Our Artillery has been very active.	
	25-7-16		Last night LOOS was heavily shelled for some hours with 4.2's + 5.9's the ENCLOSURE drew a lot of attention but no damage was done. 2/Lt Strokely took over 3 guns from MAROS right section moved them into B. KEEP W. LOOS defences. When this party was moving into LOOS a shell landed in the trench causing the following casualties:- No 28996 Pte FARRELL. A. KILLED No 29043 Pte HEALY. S, No 29699. Pte SMYTHE. G, No 29076 Pte McATEER. J. No 29078 L.Cpl Duffy. P. WOUNDED. TOTAL 1. KILLED, 4 WOUNDED. Enemy Rifle Gr Snipers, Machine Guns, Trench Mortars & Artillery	

WAR DIARY
or
INTELLIGENCE SUMMARY

(Erase heading not required.)

Army Form C. 2118.

Place	Date	Hour	Summary of Events and Information	Remarks and references to Appendices
LES BREBIS	23-7-16		were very busy in LOOS & Infantry had a lot of casualties. Weather fine. But Working Parties out day & night.	
	24-7-16		Snipers & Machine Guns very active in LOOS all night. ENEMY Artillery very active in MAROC sector. Two guns with enemy M.G. or T.M. emplacement reported on Northern parapet at M5C/3&. Two guns with trench mortar opened rapid fire on this parapet & at 11/30 flashes were obtained. Both guns opened rapid silenced the enemy using the plan. Enemy artillery was very active in LOOS. Our artillery was very active all day. Weather fine. Our M.G's very active. Working Parties on dugouts & emplacements.	
	25-7-16		Enemy Artillery, T. Mortars, Rifle Grenades etc very active in LOOS day & night, enemy in MAROC very quiet. Weather very fine. Our Artillery very active. Working Parties on dugouts & emplacements.	
	26-7-16		ENCLOSURE in LOOS very heavily Enemy Machine Guns & Snipers were very active during the night. The half day Machine gunners relieved the half day men in bullets at 5 P.M. During this No. H 35th PTE GARDNER W.E. was wounded (this man is attached for duty) 20th 28th Middlesex Regt. (to B KEEP P.W. LOOS DEFENCES and not take place as they had not come from the 32nd DIVISION did not get their guns up tonight. Weather very fine. Rained all night.	
	27-7-16		An effort has been made to get British men in LOOS trenches without overcoats. The men wring letters might had a BATH + clean clothes at 9 P.M. twenty Artillery, Snipers, Machine guns etc have been very active today & night in LOOS. B KEEP W. LOOS DEFENCES were relieved at 10.30 P.M. Working parties on emplacements & dugouts. Weather fine.	
	28-7-16		Enemy very active in LOOS Sector day & night with Artillery, Machine guns, Snipers, Rifle Grenades, Trench Mortars etc. The emplacements in LOOS sector are very poor & a lot of work will have to be done on platform to being made to break snipers. M.G's etc. How guns are along a lot of Bonly. The 3 teams which had a BATH + CLEAN cloths. The enemy's parapet opposite men wanted for work party on Dugouts + Emplacements. District 5.15 P.M. to TAUBE dropped 2 bombs & Killed 2 Otherio Infantry in building 100 yds from our office. LES BREBIS was shelled with Shrapnel + High Explosives between the hours of 10.30 P.M. + 11.30 P.M.	
	29-7-16		Weather very fine. Enemy artillery very active about 1 a.m. to 2.30 a.m. The usual activity in LOOS. Snipers + M.G's in particular were very busy. Our R.2 emplacement LOOS sector was hit by several M.G. shells but	

Army Form C. 2118.

WAR DIARY
or
INTELLIGENCE SUMMARY
(Erase heading not required.)

Instructions regarding War Diaries and Intelligence Summaries are contained in F.S. Regs., Part II. and the Staff Manual respectively. Title Pages will be prepared in manuscript.

Place	Date	Hour	Summary of Events and Information	Remarks and references to Appendices
LES BREBIS	29-7-16		No. 2969 Pvt. McGowen F. was slightly wounded in the hand by a sniper in LOOS. No damage was done.	
	30-7-16		The weather very fine. Our artillery was very active at 10 p.m. Enemy were very active in LOOS all day with artillery & at night Lighters & machine guns been very busy. We retaliated with a most unusual amount of Trench Mortars, Stoke's Guns & Rifle Grenades. Our M.G's have been very active on Dumps, Cross Rds. etc.	
	31-7-16		Weather very fine & very warm. Enemy has been very active at LOOS but is very quiet in hadu. Our M.G's are very active & tonight we have six guns doing Indirect fire on N1.C 5/5 & H.32 d 3/3. New emplacements are at present under construction & an organised shoot with 4 Vickers Guns & 6 Lewis guns will take place in Sh. 2d/Aug.16	

J H Weaver 2/Lt. OC
OC 121 Machine Gun Company.
31/7/16

Original. copy.

Vol 3

Confidential

War Diary

of

No 121 Machine Gun Company.

Machine Gun Corps.

from 1st August 1916   to   August 1916.

Volume. 3.

WAR DIARY or INTELLIGENCE SUMMARY

Army Form C. 2118.

Place	Date	Hour	Summary of Events and Information	Remarks and references to Appendices
LES BREBIS	1-8-16		The enemy have been very quiet in MAROC. In LOOS things have been quieter but the usual Sniping & Machine Gun fire has been going on. One enemy M.G has been located in the DOUBLE CRASSIER at M.4.d.8.4. & an attempt was made to knock it out. At 11 P.m. we opened fire with 3 guns & after firing three bursts the enemy gun ceased to fire. Our artillery has been very active during the night. 29093 Sgt. Q. Sheep arrived as reinforcement from Depôt & was taken on the strength. Weather very fine.	
	2-8-16		Things have been quiet up in our sector except for slight Trench Mortar & Rifle Grenade activity in LOOS. Our artillery was very active during the night. 2nd Lt. Q. L. Stockely was slightly wounded in the leg with shrapnel & was relieved by 2nd Lt. B. L. Larkin. The following reinforcements arrived from ETAPLES & were taken on the strength:- 31804 Pvnt. Dykes. H. No 31937 Pvt. Yate. H. No 35964 Pvt. Vincent. G. No 986 Pvt. Wakeling. G. Our M.G's have been very active. Word received that this Company will be relieved by 120 M.G. Coy on the 4th 8-16. Weather very fine.	
	3-8-16		The usual Trench Mortar & Rifle Grenade activity in LOOS otherwise the enemy are very quiet. We have got a most decided advantage over the enemy with our Trench Mortars, Stokes Guns etc. Our M.G's have been very active & we have succeeded in silencing the enemy at several points. We are trying to locate an enemy M.G. which enfilades "High St" LOOS & hope to put an end to this. Weather keeps very fine.	
	4-8-16		This Coy should have been relieved today but owing to our artillery activity on this evening we did not comply. The 16th Division raided enemy with a small party assisted by our artillery, French Mortars, Machine Guns etc & all transport had to be clear from LOOS by 11 P.m. so we could not get our guns back. Lt. Thomas managed to withdraw 6 guns & 2 Lt. B. L. Larkin managed to get 3 back but the other guns could not be relieved in time. The day was	

Army Form C. 2118.

WAR DIARY
or
INTELLIGENCE SUMMARY

(Erase heading not required.)

Instructions regarding War Diaries and Intelligence Summaries are contained in F.S. Regs., Part II. and the Staff Manual respectively. Title Pages will be prepared in manuscript.

Place	Date	Hour	Summary of Events and Information	Remarks and references to Appendices
LES BREBIS	4 Aug 1916		Fairly quiet. Weather was very fine.	
	5-8-16		The relief was completed in daylight. Enemy has been very quiet. All men retired from trenches in the 4-5-16 had a bath & received clean underclothes. We have taken over Reserve Line from 120 M.G. Coy & have placed 6 Guns as follows 2 in Z POINT 1 in the following C.2, C.3, C.4, C.5. 2/Lt. B.R. Larkin has been admitted to hospital sick & was evacuated to 33 C.C.S. Everything quiet. Weather fine.	
	6-8-16		The men relieved on 5th 8.16 had a bath & received issue of clean underclothes. All guns have been thoroughly overhauled, timbers repacked & everything properly cleaned. Billets were inspected & there was a thick inspection. Orders were received that the Bay proceeds to HOUCHIN on the 7th 8.16 after work i.e. 5 p.m. for 3 days training in Tactics. Everything quiet. Weather fine.	
HOUCHIN	7-8-16		Order re HOUCHIN was amended & 180 All Ranks paraded at 3 p.m. & marched to HOUCHIN arriving at 5 p.m. 10 Officers & 170 O.R.s including the Transport & limbers, 1 G.S. wagon & 1 Maltese Cart transport under Sgt. Thorogood, the whole under O.C. Bay. 2/Lt. H.A. Bullen, R.F.A. & 2/Lt. S.A. Wann Transport Officer were left at LES BREBIS with balance of Bay & 6 guns in RESERVE LINE. The Bay was billeted in tents, the Officers in tents, Baths are arranged for next morning. Weather very fine.	
	8-8-16		The following Programme (see appendix I attached below) was submitted to & approved by the 1st Infantry Bde. Steady work was carried on very successfully. Weather is very fine. Men are very keen & worked very hard. The Transport had Baths & issue of clean clothes.	Appendix I copy of Programme attached
	9-8-16		The men are working splendidly & the attached men have come on very well	

2449 Wt. W14957/M90 759,000 1/16 J.B.C. & A. Forms/C.2118/12.

Army Form C. 2118.

WAR DIARY
or
INTELLIGENCE SUMMARY
(Erase heading not required.)

Instructions regarding War Diaries and Intelligence Summaries are contained in F. S. Regs., Part II. and the Staff Manual respectively. Title Pages will be prepared in manuscript.

Place	Date	Hour	Summary of Events and Information	Remarks and references to Appendices
HOUCHIN	9-8-16		indeed the attached officers are making very great progress. The transport have greatly improved & turned out very smart & clean. The weather is splendid & the men all enjoying the change. Things are very quiet at LES BREBIS.	
LES BREBIS	10-8-16		After 10 days programme was completed the Bty marched back to LES BREBIS & arrived at 9.30pm. The weather was much cooler, much wet & light showers of rain. No 9430 Dvr McCarthy M. was wounded in the hand by splinter of shell & was evacuated to C.C.S. Everything has been very quiet. Weather has improved toward evening.	
	11-8-16		Relief's orders received at 8 a.m. that we relieve 120 M.G. Coy in MAROC at 1 P.M. Relief complete 12 midnight. Lectr has been changed over now & we came over as our first tooth over from 2nd M.G. Coy. We have now 15" Guns in the line. Dvr McBride for instructional purposes No 10038 Dvr T. Hillender & No 29009 to Dvr Pierce M. returned from M.G. School at CAMIERS. Everything quiet. Weather fine.	
	12-8-16		Every man not on duty in trenches is on working parties we have only 4 officers camp & with instruction class 2/Lt. Seagn YP B, 13th Yorkshire Regt. has been attached to this bty for duty to replace 2/Lt. O.T. Stocky wounded. Enemy very quiet. The 119th Bde in CALLONNE night carried out a small raid on enemy trenches. No 14241 Dvr Bridgell. A.G. attached from the 20th Middlesex Regt has cold shoes.	
	13-8-16		We have 2 working parties doing work in trenches & they are making excellent results on Dugouts, these parties work in 3 shifts of 8 hour each. Our artillery has been very active. The enemy are very quiet except for a few trench Mortars.	

2449 Wt. W14957/M90 750,000 1/16 J.B.C. & A. Forms/C.2118/12.

Army Form C. 2118.

WAR DIARY
or
INTELLIGENCE SUMMARY
(Erase heading not required.)

Instructions regarding War Diaries and Intelligence Summaries are contained in F. S. Regs., Part II. and the Staff Manual respectively. Title Pages will be prepared in manuscript.

Place	Date	Hour	Summary of Events and Information	Remarks and references to Appendices
LES BREBIS	13-8-16		4 Rifle Grenades on Queen St & Borehole Alley No. 26887 Pvt. W.E. Stoddworth slightly wounded with shell splinter in face. Weather very fine.	
	14-8-16		Our Artillery has been very active. Work in the trenches is progressing very well. Signal Sgt. G. Raleigh returned from hospital reported for duty. No 37th Signal Sgt. H. Green Reinforcements arrived from Etaples reported for duty. No. 16743 Pvt. J. Stow, 6503 Pvt. J. Porter, No. 18407, Pvt. Gardiner & No. 4456 Pvt. G. Gurlean. The enemy have been very active with trench mortars, aerial darts etc. Our Machine Guns have been very active. Weather unsettled. Frequent showers of rain.	
	15-8-16		Enemy artillery has been very active & shelled LES BREBIS at 2 p.m. & 6 p.m. doing a fair amount of damage to property. There were 19 soldiers killed & 29 wounded. Also about 15 civilians killed & wounded. Others were a few miles killed, in all about 50 shells were fired all H.E. about 4.2 & 5.9. Our Artillery retaliated also and Trench Mortars, Stokes & Machine Guns etc. Weather very uncertain frequent showers.	
	16-8-16		All men not doing duty in the trenches were paid today. Work in the trenches is progressing very favourably. Our artillery has been very active all day & night aided by Trench Mortars, Stokes & Machine Guns. Enemy very quiet. Weather good.	
	17-8-16		Enemy very quiet. Our Machine Guns have been very active from subrovate firing has been done by Back Billets at M.18.a & M.18.b. Pivots Rds & Dumps at M.14.a.8.3 & M.11.a.8.0. In all 10 guns were firing. All men resting have to turn out on working parties & work is progressing, rock laboriously. Orders have received that the spare Guns to be sent up to occupy new emplacements in PALL MALL. All our 16 Guns are now in the line. Weather stormy.	
	18-8-16		Our Machine Guns are very active & we fire 10 every night on Back Billets	

Army Form C. 2118.

WAR DIARY or INTELLIGENCE SUMMARY

(Erase heading not required.)

Place	Date	Hour	Summary of Events and Information	Remarks and references to Appendices
LES BREBIS	18-8-16		Cross Rds, Dumps etc. Rifle Grenades in KING St., CORDIALE AVEN, QUEEN St. vicinity. The enemy keep very active with Trench Mortars & Rifle Grenades in KING St. attached Offrs. have returned to their Battns. as we have no gun for instructional purposes. The men in trenches will be relieved 19-8-16 by other half Bn. at present in Billets. Orders received to recall guns from PALL MALL. Weather fine	
	19-8-16		All men going into the trenches have been fitted with new clothing & were paid. The relief was carried out by 4.30pm & all men from trenches had a hot change of underwear. Enemy very quiet. Our artillery very active. Received a new draft of CAMERIERS to replace 2/Lt. I.F.L. BOURNE has been posted to this Bn. to replace 2/Lt 2 stock. by 4/1 wounded. Weather very fine. As much clothing as possible was issued to men from trenches. The morning's enemy planes were over here & were chased back. There was a general clearing up & kit Inspection. The 16th Div. in LOOS made a raid with 2/Lt. J.L. Bourne & 2/Lt. H.J. Strover arrived reported to this bn. for duty. Our co-operation MGs from this Bde co-operated received that 2nd Lt. G.F. Lamb will be evacuated to England. Enemy quiet. Conditions normal. Weather fine.	
	20-8-16		All men in Billets were paid. Attached men received new clothing from their Battns. The new offrs. went into the trenches for instruction. Our M.G's have been very active on enemy Billets, Roads, Dumps etc. Our Artillery has been active. The dug out at S4 has now been completed shelter over enemy fairly quiet. Weather very fine.	
	21-8-16		Our artillery has been very active & some heavy guns have been firing at unusual or intervals day & night. New officers took their in trenches all day for instruction. Work in progress being synchronously. Our M.G's are very active 10 guns firing on back Billets, Dumps, etc. A raid was carried out by	
	22-8-16			

2449 Wt. W14957/M90 750,000 1/16 J.B.C. & A. Forms/C.2118/12.

WAR DIARY
or
INTELLIGENCE SUMMARY

(Erase heading not required.)

Army Form C. 2118.

Instructions regarding War Diaries and Intelligence Summaries are contained in F.S. Regs., Part II. and the Staff Manual respectively. Title Pages will be prepared in manuscript.

Place	Date	Hour	Summary of Events and Information	Remarks and references to Appendices
LES BREBIS	22/8/16		120th Infantry Bde in M.21.a.05.07. Enemy are very quiet. Aeroplanes passed over enemy trenches. About 6.30 p.m 19 of our were taken on the strength. The following men from Cannies No. 3969 Pvt. Phillips & No. 45922 Pvt. Stanton C. No. 45283. Pvt. Snelston D. No. 45276. Pvt. Young J. About 6 p.m No. 24744 Pvt. Richardson A. was accidentally wounded, this man was attached from 13th Yorks Rgt. Weather fine	
	23/8/16		Enemy very quiet. Two officers have gone into trenches for 24 hours instruction. They are employed at PALL MALL is now finished & has been taken over by M.G.'s are very active. 1 guns was firing in Back Billets at M.11.c. & d. M.12.c. tail brass Rd at M.12.a. 1.3. M.12 to 14.4. M.10.d.73. Our artillery is very active. Weather keeps very fine.	
	24/8/16		2/Lt Stockley O.L. has reported for duty from Corps Rest Stat. LABOUVERIE was taken on the strength. Inspected Hunded, Transport lines & Billets. Our artillery has been very active. The enemy shelled Roads behind LES BREBIS with Shrapnel & H.E. Our M.G's are very active 10 guns firing in Roads, Sumps & Trenches. Change in weather slight showers. Conditions normal enemy very quiet.	
	25/8/16		Enemy very quiet. Work is progressing very favourably. Our M.G's have been very active + 10 guns used firing on trenches & Back Billets. Enemy transport on the LENS Rd was very heavy, also during the night a relief must have been very good as no more transport was heard. The wire has not been repaired. Shelling active. Weather is again good.	
	26/8/16		Our artillery is very active. The tally boy at present in billets will relieve the men in the Trenches tomorrow 2/Lt A.B Seagut 13th Yorks Rgt. has returned to his Regt & 2/Lt Bowne has taken his place in the trenches. Our M.G's are very active & a wiring party was dispersed. Transport is very quiet tonight. We had	

Army Form C. 2118.

WAR DIARY
or
INTELLIGENCE SUMMARY
(Erase heading not required.)

Instructions regarding War Diaries and Intelligence Summaries are contained in F. S. Regs., Part II. and the Staff Manual respectively. Title Pages will be prepared in manuscript.

Place	Date	Hour	Summary of Events and Information	Remarks and references to Appendices
LES BREBIS.	26/8/16		10 Guns firing on PUITS 11 & PUITS 16. Enemy very quiet. Weather fine.	
	27/8/16		The 13th Yorks carried out a raid on the Yanckin Triangle at M.5.C. The halfcoy in Brebis relieved the 2 Coy in trenches relief complete at 4.30 p.m. No 18409 Pte GARVIN was slightly wounded. Our MG's dispersed enemy wiring party, were not yet repaired. Enemy very quiet. Weather very fine.	
	28/8/16		The Billeting arrangements have been re-organised & we have received orders to move our Billets to another part of LES BREBIS. SECTION "E" where M.G. Coys, Trench Mortars are have to stay. Men relieved from trenches have been issued with new clothes. All men in Billets are having a general cleanup. Our M.G.S. are very active & 10 guns fired on Billets at M.10.d.1 & M.11.a. for 3 hours. Enemy quiet. Weather fine.	
	29/8/16		The men in Billets are making new cookhouse & latrines at new Billets before moving in. Our M.G.S. were very active 10 guns firing at enemy Dumps, Cross Roads Back Billets until midnight & then concentrated on gaps in enemy wire made earlier in the evening by our Bangalore Torpedoes during successful raid by them. The weather has changed we have had very heavy rain with thunder & lightning. Our artillery has been very active. Enemy quiet.	
	30/8/16		Tonight the 190th Infantry Bde 13th Div take over the CALLONE SECTION from the 40th DIVISION. Weather very wet & a considerable amount of rain has fallen. There received from Bde. a BARNETT OPTICAL SIGHT for testing Ypres. We have 10 guns firing on Roads & Cross Rds at M.10.c.6.2. M.11. a.8.0 & M.12.a.1.3. We have moved old officers Billets, Orderly Room & officers Mess into the new area. Our artillery is still very active. Enemy very quiet.	
	31/8/16		Enemy very quiet. Our artillery has been very active. Work on new Billets	

Army Form C. 2118.

WAR DIARY
or
INTELLIGENCE SUMMARY

(Erase heading not required.)

Instructions regarding War Diaries and Intelligence Summaries are contained in F. S. Regs., Part II. and the Staff Manual respectively. Title Pages will be prepared in manuscript.

Place	Date	Hour	Summary of Events and Information	Remarks and references to Appendices
LES BREBIS	31/8/16		is progressing favourably. 10 guns fired on Gaps in wire, Bros Pole & Sumps By 3 guns silenced an enemy M.G. at M.S.C. Weather has been very fine. D.5 Patridge left this morning for a course of bold shooting at ABBEVILLE. Casualties Nomal.	

LES BREBIS
31-8-16.

J. Mathison. Capt.
O.C. 121 M. G. Coy.

App I

From O.C.
    121 Machine Gun Coy.

To. Headquarters
    121 Infantry Bde.

    I beg to report arrival of 121 M.G. Coy at HOUCHIN CAMP about 6 P.M. 7-8-16.

    After looking over the ground available for training, I beg to submit the attached Programme of work for 8, 9 & 10th Aug 1916.

    Trusting this will meet with your approval

HOUCHIN
8th Aug 1916.

P. Mathisen Capt
O.C. 121 M.G. Coy.

Programme of Work.
8th Aug 1916.

6 a.m.   Reveille

6.30 a.m.   Physical Drill

9 a.m.   BATHS (25 men per 30 minutes)
Remainder, Gun Drill, Rifle Drill & Semaphore.

11.30 a.m.   Officers Baths

9 a.m.   Officers Instructional Class

1.45 a.m.   Gun Drill.

to.   Limber Drill

5. P.M.   Limber Packing.

6.30 P.M.   Lecture.
ALLOCATION of DUTIES.

Programme of Work
9th AUG. 1916.

6 AM. Reveille.

6.30 AM. Physical Drill.

8.45 AM. Invisibility & Use of Cover.

to. Advanced Gun Drill.

12.30 PM. Training for Drivers.

2. PM. Movement of Guns in the Field in Open & Scrub country
to.
5. PM.
6. PM.   LECTURE.
     Fire Orders.

Programme of "Work.
10th Aug. 1916.

6.am   Reveille.

6.30 am Physical Drill.

8.45 am Special Training for N.C.O's
         (taking charge of guns in field)
to.   Special Training for Drivers

12.30 pm. Use of Telescope & Field Glasses

2. P.M. Laying Guns for Indirect &
         Night Firing.
to.   Indication & Recog of Targets

5. P.M. Combined Drill.

6.30 P.M. LECTURE
         Fire Direction

Range takers to make every use
of their instruments

Confidential Original Copy

Vol 4

"War Diary

of

121st Machine Gun Company

Machine Gun Corps.

from 1st Sept 1916 to 30th Sept 1916.

Volume 3.

Army Form C. 2118.

WAR DIARY
or
INTELLIGENCE SUMMARY.
(Erase heading not required.)

Instructions regarding War Diaries and Intelligence Summaries are contained in F. S. Regs., Part II. and the Staff Manual respectively. Title pages will be prepared in manuscript.

Place	Date	Hour	Summary of Events and Information	Remarks and references to Appendices
LES BREBIS	1/9/16		The enemy shelled LES BREBIS with about 20 H.E. shells. Results Nil. Work on Billets is progressing favorably. Our M.G's have been very active firing on, Gaps in wire, Billets & Roads. Weather very good.	
	2/9/16		Our artillery has been very active today. Work is progressing very well. Men in Billets had Bath & clean clothes. 10 Guns again fired on, Men in wire, Dumps, Cross Roads etc. Our gun's silenced enemy M.G's. Enemy very quiet. Our aircraft are very busy. 2/Lt Bain left with Lt Off. I. Clark for M.G. course at CAMERIES. Weather very fine.	
	3/9/16		Enemy very quiet. Our artillery very active all day from 8 to 10 p.m bombarded enemy trenches. Our M.G's kept very active 10 Guns firing on, Gaps in wire, Roads, Billets etc. Orders received that 120 M.G. Coy will relieve us at 2 p.m 4/9/16. Weather fine.	
	4/9/16		We were relieved today by 120 M.G. Coy we are to get 4 days rest in Billets. Work on Billets progressing. Our artillery has been very active. Weather changeable.	

Army Form C. 2118.

WAR DIARY
or
INTELLIGENCE SUMMARY.
(Erase heading not required.)

Place	Date	Hour	Summary of Events and Information	Remarks and references to Appendices
LES BREBIS	5/9/16		The Bdy had Baths & issue of clean underclothing. O.C. Bdy inspected Transport. Bdy moved into new Billets. Limbers & Equipment were cleaned & thoroughly overhauled. Our artillery very active. Enemy very quiet. Weather very wet.	
	6/9/16		The Bdy has been carrying on training. Commenced work on new Billets & may very great progress. Our artillery has been very active. Weather fine.	
	7/9/16		The enemy is very quiet. Bdy carrying on training. Work on Billets getting on very rapidly. Our artillery is very active. Enemy very quiet. Weather very fine.	
	8/9/16		The Bdy training is going on & all Limbers have been overhauled. Work on Billets is making great strides. Our artillery keeps very active. Enemy very quiet. Weather very fine.	
	9/9/16		The Bdy is in splendid shape & training is still going on. Improvements on Billets are progressing very rapidly. Our artillery keeps very active. Relief orders were received	

WAR DIARY or INTELLIGENCE SUMMARY

Army Form C. 2118.

Place	Date	Hour	Summary of Events and Information	Remarks and references to Appendices
LES BREBIS	9/9/16		Were taken over from 119 M.G. Coy in LOOS. Enemy quiet. Weather fine.	
	10/9/16		The day the relieved the 119 M.G. Coy in LOOS with 11 guns. Work is progressing very rapidly. Enemy quiet. Weather fine.	
	11/9/16		The relief was completed at 2.30 a.m. A party of 4 N.C.O.s + 50 men have been sent to Billets in LOOS as a working party under R.E. Work on Billets is now very slow. Enemy shelled LES BREBIS from 10 to 11 p.m. with 21 H.E. shells of which 8 were duds. Weather good but dull.	
	12/9/16		Enemy very quiet. Work in trenches progressing favourably. Work is still progressing on Billets & transport lines. Our artillery & trench mortars are very active. Our M.G.s fired on Back Billets & Dumps. Weather fair.	
	13/9/16		Enemy very quiet. Working parties in LOOS are busy on dug-outs & emplacements for LEWIS gunners. Work on Billets is progressing favourably. Our artillery very active. Our M.G.s very active firing on Dumps, Back Billets. Weather fair.	

Army Form C. 2118.

WAR DIARY
or
INTELLIGENCE SUMMARY.
(Erase heading not required.)

Place	Date	Hour	Summary of Events and Information	Remarks and references to Appendices
LES BREBIS	14/9/16		The Divisional Sanitary Officer inspected our new kitchens, Washhouse, latrines etc & has appointed them as the Model set for the Division. Work on Billets is still progressing. Enemy are very quiet. Our M.G's are very active on Billets above Rat. Pit. R.J. Stockly has gone into hospital sick. Leave has been opened for the Bde, commencing tomorrow. Every quiet. 2 men have to go to Base as they are under age. Weather fine.	
	15/9/16		The enemy are given to our Trumps Billets & Orrs Rds. The artillery is very active on enemy front line & rear. The Bde General inspected our Billets & was very pleased with them & stated they are the Best he has seen in France. No 29062 Pvt. J.J. Hyndl + No 25002 L.Bjs Hunnicliffe left for the Base & have been struck off the strength. The O.C. Boy goes on leave from 18th to 28th Septr. 1916. Weather fine.	
	16/9/16		The enemy has been very quiet but commenced shelling between MAROC & LES BREBIS about 12 midnight but did no	

2353 Wt. W2544/1454 700,000 5/15 D. D. & L. A.D.S.S.Forms/C. 2118.

Army Form C. 2118.

WAR DIARY
or
INTELLIGENCE SUMMARY.

(Erase heading not required.)

Instructions regarding War Diaries and Intelligence Summaries are contained in F. S. Regs., Part II. and the Staff Manual respectively. Title pages will be prepared in manuscript.

Place	Date	Hour	Summary of Events and Information	Remarks and references to Appendices
LES BREBIS	16/9/16		damage. Our artillery replied & bombarded enemy lines vigorously. 1 hour. 2 Other Ranks were slightly wounded but are at duty. Work is progressing very rapidly. Weather fair.	
	17/9/16		The O.C. has now been officially placed in charge of all Lewis Guns in the Bde. 2/Lt. J Bonne has been admitted to hospital sick. The enemy are very quiet. Our M.G's have been very active. Our artillery has again been very active. Weather very fine.	
	18/9/16		The V.O.C. left this morning for England on leave from 18th to 28th inclusive. Enemy very quiet. Our artillery + M.G's have been very active. Work is progressing very rapidly. Weather very fine.	
	19/9/16		Enemy very quiet. Our M.G.s fired on Boss Pos. + Back Billets during the night. Work or dugouts in progressing very well + another new Vickers Battle Emplacement has been commenced. Weather fine.	
	20/9/16		Enemy very active with Rifle Grenades otherwise very quiet. Our Artillery + M.G's were very active during the night. Work on	

WAR DIARY or INTELLIGENCE SUMMARY

Army Form C. 2118.

Place	Date	Hour	Summary of Events and Information	Remarks and references to Appendices
LES BREBIS	20/9/16.		Billets, Dugouts & new emplacement is progressing very rapidly. Weather very wet, raining most of the day.	
	21/9/16.		Enemy very quiet in trenches but sent 3 shells into LES BREBIS about 7.30 p.m. this did no damage. Our M.G's were again very active firing on Back Billets & Dumps. Weather still bad, very showery.	
	22/9/16.		Enemy very quiet. 3 enemy aircraft came over LES BREBIS & were driven back by our aeroplanes & anti aircraft guns. Work progressing very well. Our M.G's were very active. Weather fair.	
	23/9/16.		Our Trench Mortars were very active on enemy trenches. Enemy are keeping very quiet. Our M.G's were again very busy & Indirect Fire was carried out during the night. No. 32814 Pvt Woodage was admitted in Hospital. 2/Lt. A.R.M. Bain, Yeolyo Black & Pvt Bransford returned from M.G. course at CAMIERS. Weather fine. Enemy quiet. Our drilling has been very active. Work on Billets, Dugouts & new emplacement is progressing favorably.	
	24/9/16.			

WAR DIARY or INTELLIGENCE SUMMARY

Army Form C. 2118.

Place	Date	Hour	Summary of Events and Information	Remarks and references to Appendices
LES BREBIS	24/9/16		Our M.G's very active during the night. Weather very fine.	
	25/9/16		The enemy artillery was very active about 11 a.m. & shelled the Reserve Trenches. Our Artillery retaliated on enemy front line during the night. Our M.G's were very active on gaps in enemy wire. Work is progressing very rapidly. Weather fine.	
	26/9/16		The 20th Middlesex Regt. made a very successful raid on enemy trenches South of SEAFORTH CRATER. One German officer was killed & the body brought in & much valuable information was obtained from documents found in his possession. One T. Mortar bombarded enemy lines with good results. Information has been received that enemy are very active in front of the Loos Salient & that massed transport was seen moving behind their lines on Roads. No 29013 Pte. A/Sgt. Murphy D. _____ was tried for Drunkenness by F.G.C.M. & found Guilty & sentenced to be reduced to Private. Work has been progressing very favourably on Billets, Dugouts & new emplacement. Our M.G's	

WAR DIARY
or
INTELLIGENCE SUMMARY.

(Erase heading not required.)

Army Form C. 2118.

Place	Date	Hour	Summary of Events and Information	Remarks and references to Appendices
LES BREBIS	26/9/16		were very active during the night. About M.G. B.S.S.S. The enemy tried to occupy the craters but were repulsed with loss with our M.G. in position at foot of LOOS CRASSIER. Weather very fine.	
	27/9/16		Enemy shelled inclosure with 4.2 H.E. Our artillery retaliated. M.G's fired on gaps in wire during the night. Work is progressing rapidly. Weather fine.	
	28/9/16		Enemy T. Mortars were more active than usual. Our M.G's were very active on gaps in wire, Dumps & loose Pds. Work on trench trgwk, Emplacement & our Billets is progressing. Weather fine.	
	29/9/16		Enemy very quiet. Our artillery & M.G's very active during night. O.C. returned from leave. Work is progressing on stables & horse standings. Weather very fine.	
	30/9/16		Enemy very quiet. Our artillery & M.G's very active during the night. Work on Billets, Dugouts, new emplacement & stables is being pushed on with. Weather fine.	

Mathews Capt.
O.C. 121 M.G. Coy.

Original copy.

VOL 5

Confidential

"War Diary.

of

121 Machine Gun Coy.
Machine Gun Corps.

from :— to. 31st October 1916.

1st October. 1916. Volume. H.

Army Form C. 2118.

WAR DIARY
or
INTELLIGENCE SUMMARY.
(Erase heading not required.)

Instructions regarding War Diaries and Intelligence Summaries are contained in F. S. Regs., Part II. and the Staff Manual respectively. Title pages will be prepared in manuscript.

Place	Date	Hour	Summary of Events and Information	Remarks and references to Appendices
LES BREBIS	1st Oct 1916.		Enemy very quiet. Men in Billets & working party in trenches were paid today & had a Bath with change of clean clothing. 2/Lt. R.H. Wedrew was promoted Lieutenant with seniority from 1st April 1916. Work at Stables, Billets & in trenches progressing favourably. Weather very fine.	
	2nd Oct 1916.		Enemy very quiet. Our M.G's have been very active. Work is progressing very favourably. 2/Lt. P.L. Strickley has returned to duty from Rest camp at "AIRE". The following promotions have come through. 2/Lt. P.L. Strickley to be Lieutenant with seniority to date from 6th July 1916. Capt. O. Mathisen to be Major with seniority from 11th Sept 1916. 2/Lt. A.R. Hale has been admitted to hospital sick. Weather very fine.	
	3rd Oct 1916.		Enemy very quiet. Our aeroplanes have been very active. Our M.G's have been very active. No.14428 L/Cpl. Thos. Dott Middlesex Regt attached was seriously wounded by shell fire. Last night a successful raid was carried out on enemy trenches	

2353 Wt. W2544/1454 700,000 5/15 D. D. & L. A.D.S.S. Forms/C. 2118.

Army Form C. 2118.

WAR DIARY
or
INTELLIGENCE SUMMARY.
(Erase heading not required.)

Instructions regarding War Diaries and Intelligence Summaries are contained in F. S. Regs. Part II. and the Staff Manual respectively. Title pages will be prepared in manuscript.

Place	Date	Hour	Summary of Events and Information	Remarks and references to Appendices
LES BREBIS	3rd Oct 1916.		& at least 5 enemy were killed & numerous identifications were secured also 2 enemy M.G. emplacements were destroyed. Work progressing favourably. Weather changeable.	
	4 Oct 1916.		Enemy very quiet. Our M.G's have been very active. New open emplacement has been started on side of SEAFORTH CRATER. Work is progressing favourably. Weather unsettled. No. 15295 PTE. MYSON. W.C. seriously wounded by shell fire.	
	5/10/16.		Enemy very quiet. Work on transport lines, billets & new battle emplacements are progressing very favourably. The new open & new battle emplacements are progressing very well. 12903 Pte Callaghan J. has been seriously wounded by shell fire. Our M.G's are very active. Weather fine.	
	6/10/16		Weather has been dull. Work is progressing favourably. The men in trenches on the guns are being relieved 2 teams as a time & coming back to billets for bath, change of clothes & pay. We have now 2 open guns in LOOS in case of Indian attack	

Army Form C. 2118.

WAR DIARY
or
INTELLIGENCE SUMMARY.
(Erase heading not required.)

Place	Date	Hour	Summary of Events and Information	Remarks and references to Appendices
LES BREBIS	6/10/16		Our M.G's are very active. Enemy very quiet. No. 30664 L/Cpl Freeman J.B. returned to duty from Hospital was taken on the strength.	
	7/10/16		Enemy very quiet. Our M.G's have been very active. Work is progressing favourably. The 13th Yorks Regt had a raid & captured 2 prisoners. Weather changeable.	
	8/10/16		Enemy has been very quiet. Tonight at 8 pm the 13th Yorks & 20th Middlesex Regts made a raid on H/tronts. Our M.G's did very excellent work. With the assistance & co-operation of the 119th Bde Bty on the right, the 120th Bde Bty on the left & the 10th Machine Gun Battery we put 28 guns in action which very materially assisted the operation. Weather fair.	
	9/10/16		Weather fair. Enemy very quiet. Orders have been received that the 119th M.G. Coy will take over the Right Sector of that the 11th=10-16 & that the 121 M.G. Coy will take Loos on the 11=10-16 & that the 121 M.G. Coy will take	

2353 Wt. W2544/1454 700,000 5/15 D. D. & L. A.D.S.S. Forms/C. 2118.

Army Form C. 2118.

WAR DIARY
or
INTELLIGENCE SUMMARY.
(Erase heading not required.)

Instructions regarding War Diaries and Intelligence Summaries are contained in F.S. Regs., Part II. and the Staff Manual respectively. Title pages will be prepared in manuscript.

Place	Date	Hour	Summary of Events and Information	Remarks and references to Appendices
C/Les BREBIS	9/10/16		over the Right Sector of 14 B/S N the 12th 10.16. Work is progressing favourably. The following reinforcements have arrived & been taken on the strength. No 45360. Pte Bowsin's. Y. No 46552 Pte Burgess H. No 45447 Pte Betts H.	
	10/10/16.		Orders were received that the relief will take place at 3.30 a.m. The enemy is very quiet. Our M.G.S. have been very active. Weather dull but fair. The following reinforcements have arrived & been taken on the strength. No 46543. Cpl Duthy. J. & No 53291. Cpl Blyth. R. The following man has been attached to the Coy to replace Cpl Stubbs wounded No G/15796. Pte Dallison. G. & has been taken on the strength. At 3.30 a.m. 119 M.G. Coy relieved the Right Sector of 14 B/S At 10 a.m. 121 M.G. Coy took over Right Sector of L.O.S. from 120 M.G. Coy. The 20th Middlesex blew a mine about 11.30 a.m. which destroyed enemy galleries. Relief was completed at 2 p.m. Enemy very quiet. 2nd Lt. V.P.H.EMBROW	
	11/10/16.			

2353 Wt. W2544/1454 700,000 5/15 D. D. & L. A.D.S.S. Forms/C. 2118.

Army Form C. 2118.

WAR DIARY
or
INTELLIGENCE SUMMARY.
(Erase heading not required.)

Instructions regarding War Diaries and Intelligence Summaries are contained in F. S. Regs., Part II. and the Staff Manual respectively. Title pages will be prepared in manuscript.

Place	Date	Hour	Summary of Events and Information	Remarks and references to Appendices
LES BREBIS.	11/10/16		reported for Duty from CAMIERS was taken on the strength. Weather fair.	
	12/10/16		The enemy have been very quiet. Our M.G's are very active. Work in Billets & Transports is progressing favourably. Weather fine.	
	13/10/16		Our M.G's have been very active on Dumps etc. Work is progressing very favourably. Enemy very Quiet. Weather fine.	
	14/10/16		The enemy have been very Quiet. Our Artillery & M.G's have been very active. Work is progressing very rapidly. Weather fine.	
	15/10/16		Enemy very Quiet. Our M.G's have been very active on Enemy Billets, Bomb Stores, Dumps etc. No 28998 L/Cpl Sweeney Q. proceeded to M.G. School at CAMIERS for 3 weeks course. Work is progressing very well. Weather fine.	
	16/10/16		Enemy very quiet. Our M.G's have been very active on enemy Billets, Dumps & Snipers Pts. No 27704 Pte Daly J. was wounded by sniper. Work progressing very well. Weather fine.	

WAR DIARY
or
INTELLIGENCE SUMMARY.
(Erase heading not required.)

Army Form C. 2118.

Place	Date	Hour	Summary of Events and Information	Remarks and references to Appendices
LES BREBIS	17/10/16		Enemy very quiet. Our M.G's have been very active on enemy Roads, Dumps etc. Work is proceeding very rapidly. The Transport Lines etc were inspected by the Col. today. Weather fair.	
	18/10/16		Enemy very quiet. Our M.G's have been very active. Work is progressing very rapidly. Sector Orders have been received & the Division will be relieved very shortly & after a rest will proceed to some unknown destination. Weather very wet.	
	19/10/16		Enemy keeps very quiet. The 1st 600rds have returned in to convince finely by day as well as by night. Our M.G's are very active on Enemy Car Dumps Etc. Work for two Sections in Village line (V17 & V18) is now complete. Weather wet.	
	20/10/16		The working party in the trenches is cleaning C.15. Billet in LOOS I will return to LES BREBIS tomorrow. An order has been received that M.G. Coy establishment will be increased by 32 men from Battns in the Bde. Our M.G's have	

WAR DIARY
or
INTELLIGENCE SUMMARY.

(Erase heading not required.)

Army Form C. 2118.

Place	Date	Hour	Summary of Events and Information	Remarks and references to Appendices
LES BREBIS	20/10/16 21/10/16		been very active. The enemy are very quiet. Weather fair. Enemy are very quiet. Our M.G's have been very active on Dumps, Roads etc. The working party has now been withdrawn from LOOS. 2/Lt. d.O. Male has returned from Corps Rest Camp for duty & been taken on the strength. Relief Orders have been issued that this Bde will be relieved on the 27-28th Oct 1916 by the 14th Bde, 24th Div. Weather fair.	
	22.10.16		Enemy very quiet. We are relieving all gun teams in the trenches. Whilst relay so that they get Baths, clean underclothing, clothing & Equipment made up before leaving here. Our guns have been very active. Weather fine.	
	23.10.16		Enemy Quiet. Our M.G's have been very active. O.C. 14 M.G. Coy 14th Bde. 24 Div. visited all Gun position in this sector. Relief will take place on 26th/27th inst. Weather fair.	
	24/10/16		Enemy has been more active during last 24 hours with	

Army Form C. 2118.

WAR DIARY
or
INTELLIGENCE SUMMARY.
(Erase heading not required.)

Instructions regarding War Diaries and Intelligence Summaries are contained in F. S. Regs., Part II. and the Staff Manual respectively. Title pages will be prepared in manuscript.

Place	Date	Hour	Summary of Events and Information	Remarks and references to Appendices
LES BREBIS	24/10/16		M.G's and M.G's were very active on enemy dumps, Roads Corns Rds, etc. Lt B. Anderson & Gordon Highlanders T.F. has reported for duty been taken on the strength. Weather wet.	
	25/10/16		Enemy M.G's & T.M.s have been very active. All Gun Teams have been relieved, had Baths, clean cloths, new clothing etc. Every man in the Coy is now complete with clothing equip etc. Orders have been received to send Lt. Thomas to 24 M.G. Coy to be recorded in command. Weather fine.	
	26/10/16		Lt Thomas left to join 24 M.G. Coy has been struck off the strength accordingly. The 14th M.G. Coy arrived here about 3 p.m. relief was commenced at 7 p.m. & completed at 11.30 p.m. Orders have been received that we leave LES BREBIS at 10.15 a.m. 29th Oct 1916 & proceed to BRUAY. Weather fair.	
	27/10/16		The Coy had baths, clean cloths this morning. Everything pertaining to this sector has been handed over to Major Burches 14th M.G. Coy. Weather Wet.	

WAR DIARY
or
INTELLIGENCE SUMMARY.

Army Form C. 2118.

Place	Date	Hour	Summary of Events and Information	Remarks and references to Appendices
LES BREBIS	28/10/16		The Coy has been busy packing limbers & making final arrangements for the march to BRUAY. All Billets have been handed over to 14 M.G. Coy & they move in on the 29th Oct 1916. Weather fair	
BRUAY	29/10/16		The Coy marched at 9 a.m. & arrived at BRUAY 1.30 p.m. The Billets were very comfortable & all the men are in very good condition. We have received 2 mules & 1 G.S. limber increase to previous War Establishment. Weather very unsettled.	
LE TIRLET	30/10/16		The Coy marched today at 8 a.m. & arrived at LE TIRLET 1.40 p.m. The weather was very unsettled & has been very wet. The march in Battle Dress & an keeping very well. No 15474 Pvt H.G. Saban collapsed on 9 p.m. Tattoo Roll call & has been admitted to Hospital. Weather very wet.	
LE TIRLET	31/10/16		The Company remained in Billets for the day. Training was carried on with. Weather very unsettled.	

Q. Mathisen. Major.
Commanding 121 M.G. Coy.

Confidential.   Original Copy.

War Diary
of
121 Machine Gun Company.

Vol 6

from 1st November 1916 to 1st December 1916.

w/Columns 5

Army Form C. 2118.

WAR DIARY
or
INTELLIGENCE SUMMARY.
(Erase heading not required.)

Place	Date	Hour	Summary of Events and Information	Remarks and references to Appendices
LE TIRLET	1/11/16		Orders were received for the Day to march to HOUVIN - HOUVIGNEUL on the 2nd inst. Weather very unsettled. No 9626 Pr. McKiel. L. reported for duty & has been taken on the strength.	
HOUVIN - HOUVIGNEUL	2/11/16		The Bay marched at 8.30 a.m. & arrived in Billets at 1.30 p.m. No 45283 Pvt. O. Johnston & No 29085 Pvt. B. Powell were today awarded the Military Medal as per Appendices 5 Weather very wet.	Ref. Military Medal
	3/11/16		The Day remained in Billets today. Boy Training has been carried on. Orders have been received to march to BARLY on the 4th Nov 1916. Weather fair.	
BARLY	4/11/16		The Day marched at 8.30 a.m. & arrived at BARLY at 12.45 a.m. & took on Billets for the night. Orders were received that we proceed to BERNEUIL on the 5th Nov 1916. Weather very fine. 2/Lt. V.P. HEMBROW. Pvts. Edmonds & Summers in M.G. (Corps)	
BERNEUIL	5/11/16		The Bay paraded at 7.30 a.m. & moved at 7.45 a.m. for	

Army Form C. 2118.

Instructions regarding War Diaries and Intelligence
Summaries are contained in F. S. Regs., Part II.
and the Staff Manual respectively. Title pages
will be prepared in manuscript.

WAR DIARY
or
INTELLIGENCE SUMMARY.

(Erase heading not required.)

Place	Date	Hour	Summary of Events and Information	Remarks and references to Appendices
BERNEUIL	5/11/16		BERNEUIL arriving there shaking and Billets at 3.30 a.m. No 44318 Pte. Yishkin J. reported for duty. Was taken on the strength. Very windy but weather fine.	
	6/11/16		The Bay has remained in Billets today & Coy training has been resumed. No further orders re Bay have been received. Weather very wet.	
	7/11/16		No further orders re Bde have been received. The Bay is still carrying on with training. The weather is very wet.	
	8/11/16		The Bay is still occupying Billets in BERNEUIL carrying on with Coy training. Weather has been very wet.	
	9/11/16		The Bay is still in Billets at BERNEUIL. Orders have been received that a Bde Scheme will take place on the 11th inst & 8 Guns will be allotted to Batts. The following reinforcements reported here for duty. No 37956 Pte. Skit-By. J. Sackelees. No 514823. Sommega. D. No 579691. Jackson. H. No 579695. Pte. Jennings. E.	

2353 Wt. W3541/1454 700,000 5/15 D. D. & L. A.D.S.S. Forms/C. 2118.

Army Form C. 2118.

WAR DIARY
or
INTELLIGENCE SUMMARY.
(Erase heading not required.)

Instructions regarding War Diaries and Intelligence Summaries are contained in F. S. Regs., Part II. and the Staff Manual respectively. Title pages will be prepared in manuscript.

Place	Date	Hour	Summary of Events and Information	Remarks and references to Appendices
BERNEUIL	9/11/16		& No 20951 Pte Watson. J. from Hospital No 28998 L/Cpl Sweeny G. from M.G. School. Damiens & have been taken on the strength. Weather fine.	
	10/11/16		Coy training has been carried on. This Division is now in the Vth Army Area & attached to the XIII Corps. Weather Wet.	
	11/11/16		The weather has been very unsettled but Coy training has been carried on. No further orders have been received re our movement & period of stay here is very uncertain.	
	12/11/16		Coy training is still going on. & Range takers are going through a course to complete establishment. Weather fair. No 25674 Cpl W.L. Smith, 13th Yorks Regt attached to this Coy was today tried by F.G.C.M. Martial for Refusing to Obey an Order & sentenced to 3 months F.P. No 1.	
	13/11/16		The Coy training is still going on. The weather remains very uncertain colder & very damp.	
	14/11/16		Coy training is still being continued. Orders have been	

Army Form C. 2118.

WAR DIARY
or
INTELLIGENCE SUMMARY.
(Erase heading not required.)

Instructions regarding War Diaries and Intelligence Summaries are contained in F. S. Regs. Part II. and the Staff Manual respectively. Title pages will be prepared in manuscript.

Place	Date	Hour	Summary of Events and Information	Remarks and references to Appendices
BERNEUIL	14/11/16		received that Bn. moves to a new Billeting Area early on the 15th inst. Weather fine. Very cold.	
REMAISNIL	15/11/16		The Bn. received marching orders at 6.15 a.m. & moved at 9.30 a.m. for REMAISNIL arriving at 2 p.m. Weather fine but cold.	
	16/11/16		The Bn. remained in Billets today. The following reinforcements have been taken on the strength. No 3 & 319. Pt. Rymer. S. J. No 35672 Pt. Dobson. G. Orders were received that the Bn. will march to NEUVILLETTE tomorrow 17th Nov 1916. Weather fine.	
NEUVILLETTE	17/11/16		The Bn. marched at 9.30 a.m. & arrived about 11.30 a.m. taking over Billets for the night. Orders were received that the Bn. will march to SUS-ST-LEGER tomorrow 18-11-16. Weather fine.	
SUS-ST-LEGER	18/11/16		The Bn. marched at 11.30 a.m. & arrived here about 2.15 p.m. taking over Billets. The weather has been very bad, wet & very cold. 2 O.R's proceeded on leave.	
	19/11/16		The Bn. remained in Billets. The usual Church	

Army Form C. 2118.

WAR DIARY
or
INTELLIGENCE SUMMARY.
(Erase heading not required.)

Place	Date	Hour	Summary of Events and Information	Remarks and references to Appendices
SUS-ST-LEGER.	19/11/16		Parades were attended. Lt. J.W. Weaver left for England on leave until the 30-11-16. Weather fine.	
	20/11/16		The Coy remained in Billets. Coy training was carried on. Weather Dull & very cold.	
	21/11/16		The Coy remained in Billets. & small Tactical scheme was carried out. Orders have been received that the Coy moves 22/11/16 to FRESCHEVILLERS. Weather very cold, damp, very foggy.	
AUTHIEULE	22/11/16		The Coy marched at 8.30 a.m. & en route Coy's destination has been changed to AUTHIEULE, where we arrived at 1.45 a.m. 2/Lt. H.J. Shrive returned to ENGLAND on duty. Orders were received that Coy moves to HALLOY on the 23-11-16. Weather fair.	
HALLOY	23/11/16		The Coy marched at 8.50 a.m. arriving HALLOY at 1.50 P.M. taking over Billets for the night. Orders were received that the Coy will move to PONT REMY on the 24-11-16.	

Army Form C. 2118.

WAR DIARY
or
INTELLIGENCE SUMMARY.
(Erase heading not required.)

Instructions regarding War Diaries and Intelligence Summaries are contained in F.S. Regs., Part II. and the Staff Manual respectively. Title pages will be prepared in manuscript.

Place	Date	Hour	Summary of Events and Information	Remarks and references to Appendices
HALLOY	23/11/16		Weather fine.	
PONT REMY	24/11/16		The Coy marched at 8.30 a.m. & arrived PONT REMY at 3/5 PM took over Billets. Weather fair.	
	25/11/16		The Coy remained in Billets. Mens kits & Equipment were inspected, Guns were overhauled & Limbers repacked. Orders were received that the Coy would move to BRUCAMPS on the 26-11-16. Weather Wet.	
BRUCAMPS	26/11/16		The Coy marched at 9 a.m. & arrived BRUCAMPS at 2.15 p.m. taking over Billets. 2/Lt. V.P.HEMBREW, Pte. Edmonds.G. No26682 Pte O'Donnell.J. No29037 & Pte Sommers.T. No29040. returned from M.G. Course at CAMIERS. Weather fine, very cold.	
	27/11/16		Orders were received that the Coy would remain here for some time that Coy training had to be carried on. Weather fine. All kits & Equipment in the Coy has been overhauled & checked.	
	28/11/16		The Coy has resumed training on lines laid down by	

Army Form C. 2118.

WAR DIARY
or
INTELLIGENCE SUMMARY.
(Erase heading not required.)

Place	Date	Hour	Summary of Events and Information	Remarks and references to Appendices
BRUCAMPS	28/11/16		The G.O.C. & Programme of Work for the week ending 2/12/16 Programme has been submitted, as per attached appendices. Weather of day training fine. Very cold.	
	29/11/16		The day training is being carried on as per attached copy of Programme. Orders have been received that all 1st Line Transport will be inspected at 12.15 pm 30-11-16 by G.O. 40th Div Train & the D.A.V.C. & that Col Clarke XV Corps M.G. Officer will inspect the day at 9.30 a.m. 30-11-16. Weather fine.	
	30/11/16		Day training was carried on. The day was inspected by Brigadier General G. Campbell & Lt. Col R.Y. Clarke, Machine Gun Officer XV Corps. All 1st Line transport was inspected by the G.O. to Div Train & the D.A.V.C. The Res. W. Thur. C. Y is attached to this day & has been taken on the strength. Weather fair.	

G Mathusing Major
O.C. 121 M.G. Coy.

I. Corps No A 56/186.

Madge's
No 2444.
1 Nov 1916.
40th Division

HEADQUARTERS
40th DIVISION.

With reference to the recommendations forwarded under your No 2441A, dated 29/10/16. The Corps Commander has under authority granted by His Majesty the King, awarded the MILITARY MEDAL to the undernamed.

The recipients should be informed where possible, and their names will be published in the London Gazette in due course.

<u>121st Machine Gun Company.</u>
   No 45283. Private O. Thristan.
   No 29085 Private C. Powell.

H.Q. I Corps.
30/10/16.

(Signed) G. N. Anderson.
Brig-General.
D.A & Q.M.G. I Corps.

2

Headquarters
121st Infantry Brigade.

For necessary action. The Major-General wishes these men to be notified as early as possible and the enclosed ribbons handed to them with his congratulations.

40th Division
1st November 1916.

Captain
D.A.A & Q.M.G.

ROUTINE ORDERS — No 164.
— By —
MAJOR-GENERAL. H.G. RUGGLES-BRISE, C.B. M.V.O.
COMMANDING 40th DIVISION.

HQRS 40th DIVISION.
1st NOVEMBER 1916.

722. MILITARY MEDAL.

The Corps Commander has awarded the Military Medal to the undermentioned for the acts of gallantry stated:—

(a) No 29085. Private Christopher Powell.
121. Machine Gun Company.

On the morning of the 26th October 1916, about 9.45 a.m. Pte C Powell observed that a gun position was being heavily bombarded by heavy T.M.S and that a direct hit had been made on this position. He immediately, on his own initiative rushed up into the sap head and there found that the Gun had been blown off the Emplacement and was buried in the trench, and that the men on the Gun had both been severely wounded and partially buried. He at once assisted the wounded men and then dug out the Gun. While Pte Powell was getting the Gun out he was blown down the side of the Crater, but returned and succeeded in recovering the Gun. During the whole of this period Pte Powell was exposed and in full view within 100 yards of the enemy and under a heavy T.M bombardment.

2

(b) N° 45283 Private. Owen. Thristan.
121st Machine Gun Company.

On the morning of the 26th October, 1916, about 9-45 a.m. Pte Thristan heard that the enemy had obtained a direct hit on the Gun position situated in a sap head on top of a mine Crater. On his own initiative he rushed up to the Gun position and found that Pte Powell had just removed the Gun. Pte Thristan immediately proceeded to search for the tripod and spare parts which he recovered and removed to another position; also 7 Belt-boxes of S.A.A.

Pte Thristan had to make several journeys up and down the Crater fully exposed to the enemy, and during the whole period the enemy were bombarding the Crater with heavy Trench Mortars. He was working in a most exposed and dangerous position for at least half an hour within 100 yds. of the enemy lines.

121 Machine Gun Company.

Programme of work for the week ending Saturday Dec 2nd 1916
Company Parade Ground will be in Field E of ruined
Church on BRUCAMPS – DOMART Road.

Day	Time	Subject	Remarks
Tuesday	6.30 to 7.0 a.m.	Physical Drill	Range Finders
Wednesday	9.0 to 10.0	Rifle Exercises	To complete Course
Thursday	10.0 to 11.0	Gun Drill	under Lt. P.L. Stockley.
	11.15 to 12.15	Stoppages	To parade with Coy for
	2.0 to 3.0 p.m.	Squad Drill	all close order drill &
	3.0 to 4.0	Firing Exercises	Rifle Exercises.
		Lectures. Discipline,	
		Characteristics,	Runners & Scouts
		Fire Orders.	Will parade with Coy
			for all close order drill
Friday	6.30 to 7.0 a.m.	Physical Drill	and Rifle Exercises.
	9.0 to 10.0	Rifle Exercises	Remainder of the time
	10.0 to 11.0	Gun Drill	they will parade under
	11.15 to 12.15	Stoppages (Blindfolded)	the Orderly Officer for
	2.0 to 3.0 p.m.	Squad Drill	instruction in Compass
	3.0 to 4.0	Elementary Tests.	and map work etc.
		Lectures	
		Points	Signallers
		before during and after	Under Cpl Roxborough
		Firing.	Training in Visual
			Signalling, Buzzer
Saturday	6.30 to 7.0 a.m.	Physical Training.	Wiring and Telephone Work
	9.0 to 10.0	Rifle Exercises.	
	10.0 to 11.0	Gun Drill.	N.C.O's ! are responsible
	11.15 to 12.15	Exam Elementary Tests	for care & cleaning
			of their Guns at
			all times

27/11/16

P. Mathisen, Major
Commanding 121 M Gun Coy.

To Hqrs
121. Inf Bde.

Herewith - Please find copy of
War diary for the
month ending 31st December
1916.

2/1/17

J.W. Warwick Major
Commanding 121 M.G.Cy

Original copy.

Confidential
War Diary
of
121 Machine Gun Coy.

Vol 7

From 1 December 1916. to. 31st December 1916.

Column. 6.

Army Form C. 2118.

WAR DIARY
or
INTELLIGENCE SUMMARY.
(Erase heading not required.)

Instructions regarding War Diaries and Intelligence Summaries are contained in F. S. Regs., Part II. and the Staff Manual respectively. Title pages will be prepared in manuscript.

Place	Date	Hour	Summary of Events and Information	Remarks and references to Appendices
BRUCAMP.	1st Dec 19/16		The Day training is going on steadily as per Programme. Orders have been received that this Div is now in the XVI Corps. The weather has been very cold, damp & foggy.	
	2/12/16		The Coy had Baths at DOMART & clean clothes have been issued. The Coy has been paid. Training is going on. Weather very cold & damp.	
	3/12/16		The Roman Catholics paraded at 9.30 a.m. Church of England paraded 10.30 a.m. Col Clarke gave O.C. Coy & the 4 Section Officers a small Tactical Scheme from 10.45 a.m. until 1.30 p.m. Lt. J.W. Weaver to Bt. Green to Ord. Junkead & to Ord. Junkead returned from leave at 11.45 p.m. Weather fair, very cold.	
	4/12/16		The Day training is being carried on as per attached Programme of work. 2/Lt V.P. HEMBROW, sick, has been evacuated to C.C.S. Weather fair.	Programme of Work attached
	5/12/16		Orders were received to amend our Programme of Work to read, Small Tactical Schemes on Thursday, Friday & Saturday	Programme of Work to for Week Ending 9/12/16.)

WAR DIARY or INTELLIGENCE SUMMARY

Army Form C. 2118.

Place	Date	Hour	Summary of Events and Information	Remarks and references to Appendices
BRUCAMP	5/12/16		Weather fair. 1 + O.R's, reinforcements from M.G. BASE DEPOT have reported for duty & been taken on the strength.	
	6/12/16		Coy Training has been carried on. Orders have been received that the Brigadier-General will inspect the Coy at 12.45 p.m. 7th Dec 1916. Weather fair.	
	7/12/16		The Training is progressing very well. The General inspected the Coy & was very pleased with the turn out. A small Tactical Scheme was carried out from 2.30 p.m. & the General expressed great satisfaction. Weather Damp & foggy.	
	8/12/16		The Coy Training has been carried on. Orders have been received that the Transport will march from here on the 10th Dec 1916 to SAILLEY LAURETTE & will proceed to the new Billeting area by road & independently from the Coy. Orders have been received that the Coy will	

Army Form C. 2118.

WAR DIARY
or
INTELLIGENCE SUMMARY.
(Erase heading not required.)

Instructions regarding War Diaries and Intelligence Summaries are contained in F. S. Regs., Part II. and the Staff Manual respectively. Title pages will be prepared in manuscript.

Place	Date	Hour	Summary of Events and Information	Remarks and references to Appendices
BRUCAMP	8/12/16		leave here on the 11th Dec & entrain for the new Billeting Area. Weather changeable wet.	
	9/12/16		The Company had Bathing at DOMART. All Limbers have been packed & Transport will leave here at 8 a.m. 10th Dec 1916 under 2/Lt S.A. WANN T.O. The Coy Q.M. Sergt. left here this morning with the Bde Advance Party to represent this Coy & to take over Stores, Billets etc in the new Area. The Coy has been paid. Weather fair.	
	10/12/16		Orders have been received that the Coy will march on 11th Dec 1916 & entrain at LONGPRE at 8 a.m. for BUIRE & then march to CAMP 125, near SAILLEY LAURETTE & take over Billets. The usual Church Services were attended by the Coy. The Transport under 2/Lt S.A. WANN. T.O. left at 8 a.m. en route for SAILLEY LAURETTE by road. Weather fair.	
SAILLEY-LAURETTE	11/12/16		The Coy was divided into two parties, the first party	

2353 Wt. W2544/1454 700,000 5/15 D. D. & L. A.D.S.S. Forms/C. 2118.

Army Form C. 2118.

WAR DIARY
or
INTELLIGENCE SUMMARY.

(Erase heading not required.)

Instructions regarding War Diaries and Intelligence Summaries are contained in F. S. Regs., Part II. and the Staff Manual respectively. Title pages will be prepared in manuscript.

Place	Date	Hour	Summary of Events and Information	Remarks and references to Appendices
SAILLEY-LAURETTE	11/2/16		entraining at 8 a.m. under O.C. Coy & the second party at 10.30 a.m. under Lt. J.W. WEAVER. 2/m.C. at LONGPRE STN. The first party arrived at 5 p.m., the second party at 4.40 p.m. & huts were taken over for the Coy. The transport arrived at 4.45 p.m. No 28823 Dr. MORE. H.J. reported him for duty from the Base & has been taken on the strength of the Coy. Weather Wet.	
	12/2/16		The Coy was made into a working party for the day arrg to the dirty & unsanitary condition of the Camp & Huts. Weather fair.	
	13/2/16		The Coy Training has been resumed. Fatigue parties have been working on new bookhouse, Roads, Horse standings & a 30 yds Range. Weather very unsettled.	
	14/2/16		Coy Training has been carried on. Work is progressing favourably. Weather Very Wet.	
	15/2/16		Coy Training has been carried on, Fatigue Parties have been working on bookhouse, Horse standings & Roads. 30 yds Range for	

Army Form C. 2118.

WAR DIARY
or
INTELLIGENCE SUMMARY.
(Erase heading not required.)

Instructions regarding War Diaries and Intelligence Summaries are contained in F. S. Regs., Part II. and the Staff Manual respectively. Title pages will be prepared in manuscript.

Place	Date	Hour	Summary of Events and Information	Remarks and references to Appendices
SAILLEY-LAURETTE	15/12/16		# Targets has been completed. Orders have been received that the Coy will move & take up new Billets in the village of SAILLEY LAURETTE on the 16th Dec 1916. Weather Wet.	
	16/12/16		The Coy paraded & moved into Billets in SAILLEY LAURETTE at 8 a.m. No 25692 L.Cpl P. Drake R. returned from M.G. Course at CAMIERS. Weather fair.	
	17/12/16		The Coy attended the usual Divine Service Parades. The Y.G.C.M. on No 11724 Pte Y.W. Rommel was promulgated the sentence was 3 months No 1 F.P. O.C. Coy has been put in charge of all Repairs on Roads in SAILLEY LAURETTE. 1 Officer & 12 O.R. have been detailed as permanent Yn Brigade. Work on the Roads is progressing & the G.O.C. has complimented the Coy on the great improvement amount of work done on the Roads. Half the Coy has carried on Swift Coy training, the remainder are on Road work. Weather Fair.	
	18/12/16			

Army Form C. 2118.

WAR DIARY
or
INTELLIGENCE SUMMARY.
(Erase heading not required.)

Instructions regarding War Diaries and Intelligence Summaries are contained in F. S. Regs., Part II. and the Staff Manual respectively. Title pages will be prepared in manuscript.

Place	Date	Hour	Summary of Events and Information	Remarks and references to Appendices
SAILLEY-LAVRETTE	19/11/16		Road work is progressing very rapidly. Half the day has carried on with the training 1/c 32071. Dr Gant. W. has been sent on a bold showing Course for brookes his attacks to 1st Coy. A.S.C. 40th Div Train. 1/c 25.693. Pte Smith. Y.H. has been sent to the Base as he is under age. No 29335 L.Cpl. G. Murry returned from Transport Course at ABBEVILLE. Weather fine.	
	20/12/16		Orders have been received that the Bde will move from here to BRAY on the 27 Dec 1916 & become Div Reserve for Right sector of XII Corps front. Work & Coy training is progressing normally. Weather fine	
	21/12/16		Lt Col General held a conference with ref to our moving into the line. No 25708. Pte L.J. Merrill left for England on leave from 22nd Dec 1916 to 1st Jan 1917. Work & Coy training is progressing. Weather fine.	
	22/12/16		The Coy has had Baths, Clean Clothes & Pay. Work	

Army Form C. 2118.

WAR DIARY
or
INTELLIGENCE SUMMARY.
(Erase heading not required.)

Place	Date	Hour	Summary of Events and Information	Remarks and references to Appendices
SAILLY-LAURETTE.	22/12/16		& Coy training is being carried on. The B.Coy General has superintended the Transport of this unit. in General Efficiency & Turn Out. See Appendix. Weather wet	Ref 3334 Appx re Transport
	23/12/16		The Coy Training is being carried on. Work is still progressing rapidly. Weather very unsettled, cold & wet.	
	24/12/16		The Coy attended the usual Divine Service. Work on Roads was resumed at 2 p.m. Weather fine very cold.	
	25/12/16		The Coy had a Holiday for Xmas Day & the officers provided Sports, Xmas Dinner. In the afternoon a Boxing Tournament was held. Sgt Ellis wining a tournament. One officer's charger was lost. Orders were received that the Coy will march to CAMP. 17. at G.9.a.2.8 Ref Map 1/40,000 ALBERT on the morning of the 27th Dec 1916 & go into Divi Reserve. Weather fine.	
	26/12/16		Work & Coy training has been resumed. Limbers have been cleaned & packed ready to march to New Billeting Area. Weather fine	

Army Form C. 2118.

WAR DIARY
or
INTELLIGENCE SUMMARY.
(Erase heading not required.)

Instructions regarding War Diaries and Intelligence Summaries are contained in F. S. Regs., Part II. and the Staff Manual respectively. Title pages will be prepared in manuscript.

Place	Date	Hour	Summary of Events and Information	Remarks and references to Appendices
CAMP 17. (SUZANNE)	27/12/16.		The Coy marched at 10.50 a.m. arriving at CAMP 17. at 4 p.m. taking over Billets. This camp is in a sea of mud & in a very dirty condition. Weather fair.	
	28/12/16		The Coy has been turned on to Road Work, trying to improve the condition of the Camp. Enemy shelled BRAY with about 20, 6 inch H.E. Shells. Weather Wet.	
	29/12/16		The Coy is still on Road Work. The O.C. Coy & Lt. C. Anderson have to go up to the trenches to have a look round before taking over from the 120 M.G. Coy on the 31st Dec 1916 & will remain for the night. Weather Wet.	
	30/12/16.		The Coy is still on Road Work. The O.C. Coy & Lt. C. Anderson returned from the trenches at 11.30 a.m. The Coy will take over from the 120 M.G. Coy at 1 p.m. on the 31st Dec 1916. Weather Wet.	
	31/12/16		The Coy left Camp 17 at 10.15 am and were conveyed by motor	

WAR DIARY
or
INTELLIGENCE SUMMARY.

Army Form C. 2118.

Place	Date	Hour	Summary of Events and Information	Remarks and references to Appendices
	31/12/16		Lorries to Road Junction at Trancrehas from whence Kay trades t Coy HQrs at Argoeuve B'17 c.0.5. Ref Map. Barchavesnes 1/10000 No 1, 2 & 3 Sections, accompanied by O.C. & C.S.M. proceeded to advanced Coy. HQrs to take over from 120 M. G. Coy at ANDOVER C.13.a.8.3.; No 1 & 2 Sections going on to relieve gun teams of that Coy. Relief complete 10.10 p.m. Casualties nil. Trenches in a very bad condition. Weather sultry & cold.	

J. H. Heanes Knt-A. Major
Commanding 121 M.G.C.

1/1/17.

121 Machine Gun Company.

Programme of Work for the week ending Saturday 16/12/16

Day	Time	Subject	Remarks
MONDAY	9.0 To 10.0 a.m.	Gun drill.	LECTURES :-
	10.0 To 11.0	Recognition & Indication of Targets	Fire direction
	11.15 To 12.15	Squad drill	Allocation of Duties.
	2.0 To 3.0	Stoppages	Indirect & Night
	3.0 To 4.0	Box Respirator drill.	Firing.
			Study of Ground.
TUESDAY	9.0 To 10.0	Bombing	RANGE FINDERS
	10.0 To 11.0	Gun drill	To complete course
	11.15 To 12.15	Rifle exercises	under Lt. Ph. Stockley.
	2.0 To 3.0	Stoppages	They will parade with
	3.0 To 4.0	Visual Training.	Coy for all close order
			drill & Rifle exercises.
WEDNESDAY	9.0 To 10.0	Gun drill	RUNNERS & SCOUTS
	10.0 To 11.0	Points before & after firing	will parade with Coy
	11.15 To 12.15	Stoppages	for all close order
	2.0 To 3.0	Use of Cover	drill & Rifle exercises.
	3.0 To 4.0	Squad Drill.	Remainder of Time
			under the Orderly Officer
THURSDAY	9.0 To 10.0	Squad drill.	for instructions in
	10.0 To 11.0	Spare parts	Map & Compass work
	11.15 To 12.15	Advanced Gun Drill	SIGNALLERS
	2.0 To 3.0	Visual Training.	Under Cpl Roxborough.
	3.0 To 4.0	Use of Cover.	Training in Visual
			Signalling, Buzzer
FRIDAY	9.0 To 10.0	Rifle exercises.	and field telephone
	10.0 To 11.0	Advanced Gun drill.	work.
	11.15 To 12.15	Use of Cover.	
	2.0 To 3.0	Bombing.	
	3.0 To 4.0	Stoppages.	
SATURDAY 9/12/16	9.0 To 12.15	Test of Elementary Training	

J. W. Weaver Lt. Major
Commanding 121 M Gun Coy.

121 Machine Gun Company.

Programme of Work for Weekending Saturday December 9th 1916

Day	Time	Sections	Subject	Remarks
MONDAY	9.0 To 12.15	No 1 Section	Firing on 30 yds. Range	Part I Table C.
"	2.0 To 3.30	"	Stoppages on 30 yds Range	
"	All day	No 2 Section	Guards & Working Parties	
"	9.0 To 10.0	No 3 & 4 Sections	Rifle exercises	
"	10.0 To 11.0	"	Stoppages with Box Respirators	
"	11.15 To 11.45	"	Bombing	
"	11.45 To 12.30	"	Recognition & Indication of Targets	
"	2.0 To 3.0	"	Gun Drill	
"	3.0 To 4.0	"	Use of Cover	
TUESDAY	9.0 To 12.15	No 2 Section	Firing on 30 yds Range	Part I Table C.
"	2.0 To 3.30	"	Stoppages on 30 yds Range	
"	All day	No 3 Section	Guards & Working Parties	
"	9.0 To 9.30	No 1 & 4 Sections	Bombing	
"	9.30 To 10.30	"	Use of Cover	
"	10.30 To 11.0	"	Visual Training	
"	11.15 To 12.30	"	Rifle Exercises	
"	2.0 To 3.0	"	Advanced Gun drill	
"	3.0 To 4.0	"	Stoppages with Box Respirators	
WEDNESDAY	9.0 To 12.15	No 3 Section	Firing on 30 yds Range	Part I Table C.
"	2.0 To 3.30	"	Stoppages on 30 yds Range	
"	All day	No 4 Section	Guards & Working Parties	
"	9.0 To 10.0	No 1 & 2 Sections	Gun drill	
"	10.0 To 11.0	"	Squad Drill	
"	11.15 To 11.45	"	Bombing	
"	11.45 To 12.30	"	Recognition & Indication of Targets	
"	2.0 To 3.0	"	Gun drill with Box Respirators	
"	3.0 To 4.0	"	Points before during & after firing	
THURSDAY	9.0 To 12.15	No 4 Section	Firing on 30 yds Range	Part I Table C.
"	2.0 To 3.30	"	Stoppages on 30 yds Range	
"	All day	No 1 Section	Guards & Working Parties	
"	9.0 To 10.0	No 2 & 3 Sections	Advanced Gun drill	
"	10.0 To 11.0	"	Use of Cover	
"	11.15 To 11.45	"	Bombing	
"	11.45 To 12.30	"	Recognition & Indication of Targets	
"	2.0 To 3.0	"	Squad Drill	
"	3.0 To 4.0	"	Rifle Exercises (Rapid Loading)	
FRIDAY	9.0 To 12.15	No 1 & 2 Sections	Gun drill and firing on Range	Advanced Drill.
"	9.0 To 10.0	No 3 & 4 Sections	Rifle Exercises	
"	10.0 To 11.0	"	Use of Cover	
"	11.0 To 11.30	"	Bombing	
"	1.0 To 4.0	"	Advanced Drill and firing on Range	
"	2.0 To 3.0	No 1 & 2 Sections	Use of Cover	
"	3.0 To 4.0	"	Squad Drill	
SATURDAY	9.0 To 12.30	All Sections	Test of Elementary Training	
"	9.0 To 12.30	Awkward Squad	Part I Table C on Range	

1/12/16.

J. W. Meanock, Major
Commanding 121 M.G. Coy.

OFFICER COMMANDING,
  12th Batt. Suffolk Regiment.
  13th Batt. Yorkshire Regiment.
  20th Batt. Middlesex Regiment.
  21st Batt. Middlesex Regiment.
  121st Machine Gun Company.

HEADQUARTERS
NO 333 G
22nd DEC 1916
121st INFANTRY BDE.

As a result of the inspection of the Brigade Transport held by the O.C., 40th Divisional Train, and A.D.V.S, the following report has been received:-

"The condition of the animals was very good and the Harness and Vehicles well kept, considering the very hard work entailed by the many marches and bad weather experienced on many occassions. The Brigade Transport appeared very workmanlike and efficient. I would like to call special attention to the Transport of the Machine Gun Company, which showed so great an improvement that I found it was quite the Best."

The Brigadier-General Commanding congratulates Commanding Officers, Transport Officers and men and particularly the Machine Gun Company, on the above Good report. He fully realises and appreciates the hard work that has led to this satisfactory Standard being reached, and has no doubt that it will be maintained and still further improved in the future.

22nd December 1916.

(Sgd.) A. L. Cowlan
Captain
Staff Captain
121st Infantry Brigade.

Original Copy.

Vol 8

Confidential

War Diary.
of
121 Machine Gun Company
Machine Gun Corps.

from 1st January 1917 to 31st January 1917.

Volume 7

Army Form C. 2118.

WAR DIARY
or
INTELLIGENCE SUMMARY.
(Erase heading not required.)

Instructions regarding War Diaries and Intelligence Summaries are contained in F. S. Regs., Part II. and the Staff Manual respectively. Title pages will be prepared in manuscript.

Place	Date	Hour	Summary of Events and Information	Remarks and references to Appendices
BOUCHAVESNES	1/1/17		Enemy artillery was very active tour artillery replied vigorously. The trenches are in an appalling state & it is impossible to get any material up for improvements. Casualties Nil. Weather fair.	
	2/1/17		Our artillery has been very active & the enemy has shelled intermittently with H.E. & Shrapnel. The 4 Lynn team's in the line have been relieved & are very fit & cheery. Casualties Nil. Weather fair.	
	3/1/17		The enemy artillery & our own artillery have both been very active, last night No 29073 Pvt. Barrow J. was relieved & sent to the Base as a Munition Worker. Casualties Nil. Weather fair.	
	4/1/17		The usual artillery activity has been going on. The 4 Lynn team's have been relieved. Reinforcements to O.Rs. reported from the Base. The weather has been very unsettled.	

Army Form C. 2118.

WAR DIARY
or
INTELLIGENCE SUMMARY.
(Erase heading not required.)

Instructions regarding War Diaries and Intelligence Summaries are contained in F. S. Regs., Part II. and the Staff Manual respectively. Title pages will be prepared in manuscript.

Place	Date	Hour	Summary of Events and Information	Remarks and references to Appendices
BOUCHAVESNES	5/1/17		The enemy artillery has been very active. The trenches are in a very bad state. New Dugouts & Emplacements have been started. Casualties No 9626. Pte McNeal G. slightly wounded 2 mules killed. Weather bad.	
	6/1/17		The gun teams were relieved. Casualties Kil. 2/Lt. A.O. Male has been evacuated to C.C.S. sick. Work is progressing on Dugouts & Empl. Weather fair.	
	7/1/17		The weather has been very wet. Enemy artillery too been very active, work is progressing favourably. Casualties Nil. Weather bad.	
	8/1/17		The Coy was relieved by the 120 M.G.Coy at 8p.m & returned to Camp 17. for 4 days rest. Casualties Nil. Weather fair, very cold.	
SUZANNE	9/1/17		The Coy has been split into two, one lot has been doing Road work & other party cleaning Guns & equipment Lt. J.W. Weaver evacuated to C.C.S. sick. Weather cold.	

2353 Wt. W3544/1454 700,000 5/15 D. D. & L. A.D.S.S. Forms/C 2118.

WAR DIARY
or
INTELLIGENCE SUMMARY.

Army Form C. 2118.

Place	Date	Hour	Summary of Events and Information	Remarks and references to Appendices
SUZANNE.	10/1/17.		The guns & equipment have been overhauled & cleaned. Reinforcements:- 8 O.R's have reported from the Base	
	11/1/17.		Half the Coy were doing Fatigue, the remainder were on the Road Work. Work has been progressing very well. Weather fair.	
	12/1/17.		The Coy marched from Camp 17 & relieved the 120th M.G. Coy in RANCOURT SECTOR. The Advanced Coy Headq'rs are at ADELPHI DUMP, near Headq'rs are at LE FOREST. Details & Transport are at MAUREPAS RAVINE. No 6 in Offord proceeded on leave from the 13/1/17 to 23/1/17. Weather good, very cold.	
RANCOURT	12/1/17.		1/30th enemy and our Artillery have been very active day & night. Work has been commenced on to two Forward M/y guns called LINK & LUCY. R.E. have nearly completed dugouts for M.G's 5 & 6. & M.G's 7 & 8. Trench stores are very low. Weather fine.	

WAR DIARY or INTELLIGENCE SUMMARY

Army Form C. 2118.

Place	Date	Hour	Summary of Events and Information	Remarks and references to Appendices
RANCOURT	14/1/17		Snow fell during the night. Work on dugout is progressing rapidly. Both our & enemy artillery have been very active. Cpt Goggin R. proceeded the M.G. School at CAMIERS for course. Weather Clear, very cold.	
	15/1/17		The Dugout for M.G. 7 & 8 in Corps line has been trucked & 2 guns have been moved into these positions. All other work is progressing. Trench stores are being made up. Enemy artillery has been very active. Weather good.	
	16/1/17		All usual working activity has been going on day & night. Work is proceeding very rapidly. Weather Good.	
	17/1/17		The enemy artillery has been very active. 9 mules were killed, 1 severely wounded & 2 horses slightly wounded by shell fire in the Transport lines at Maurepas Ravine. Work is proceeding rapidly & the Dugouts for M.G. 5 & 6 has been completed. Weather Good.	
	18/1/17		The enemy artillery is always very active on the whole	

Army Form C. 2118.

WAR DIARY
or
INTELLIGENCE SUMMARY.
(Erase heading not required.)

Instructions regarding War Diaries and Intelligence Summaries are contained in F.S. Regs., Part II. and the Staff Manual respectively. Title pages will be prepared in manuscript.

Place	Date	Hour	Summary of Events and Information	Remarks and references to Appendices
RANCOURT	18/1/17		Both front is shelled intermittently day & night. Reinforcements to O.R.s reported from the Base. Two guns have been moved into M.G.s 5 & 6 (position taken over). Work is progressing. Weather Good.	
	19/1/17		Both our shelling & enemy shelling have been very active. Work is proceeding very rapidly. Except for the shelling things are very quiet. All men are busy for very cheery. Weather fine but very cold.	
	20/1/17		The shelling activity is still going on both sides. Trench stores are being made up & moved up the Emplacements have been completed, both SAA & Bombs. Weather good, very cold.	
	21/1/17		The shelling activity is still going on both sides. Work on dugouts is going on splendidly, new emplacements are now being constructed. Weather Good. Very cold.	
	22/1/17		The Coy. has been relieved by the 119th M.G. Coy overnight	

2353 Wt. W2544/1454 700,000 5/15 D. D. & L. A.D.S.S. Forms/C. 2118.

Army Form C. 2118.

WAR DIARY
or
INTELLIGENCE SUMMARY.
(Erase heading not required.)

Instructions regarding War Diaries and Intelligence Summaries are contained in F. S. Regs., Part II. and the Staff Manual respectively. Title pages will be prepared in manuscript.

Place	Date	Hour	Summary of Events and Information	Remarks and references to Appendices
RANCOURT	22/1/17		To Camp 19. 2/LT. V.P. HEMBROW returned from Hospital. Relief complete by 8 p.m. Casualties Nil. Weather Good, very cold.	
SUZANNE	23/1/17		The Bty is moving back into Corps Reserve Area for a rest on the 25th Jan 1917. The Bty has been detailed for Road Work on roads in vicinity of Camp 17. Weather Good, very cold.	
	24/1/17		The guns & equipment have been cleaned & overhauled. Half of the Bty has been on Road Work. Weather Good, very cold.	
CHIPILLY	25/1/17		The Bty marched at 11 a.m. & proceeded to Chipilly Camp 12 arriving & taking over Billets at 3.30 P.M. Weather good, very cold.	
	26/1/17		The Bty has moved from "A" Lines Camp 12 to "C" Lines Camp 12, taking over Billets from the 25th M.G. Coy. Guns & Equipment have been overhauled. Weather good. Very cold.	

Army Form C. 2118.

WAR DIARY
or
INTELLIGENCE SUMMARY.
(Erase heading not required.)

Instructions regarding War Diaries and Intelligence Summaries are contained in F. S. Regs., Part II. and the Staff Manual respectively. Title pages will be prepared in manuscript.

Place	Date	Hour	Summary of Events and Information	Remarks and references to Appendices
CHIPILLY	27/1/17		The day training has been resumed, all ammunition & belts have been thoroughly cleaned, overhauled & refilled. The weather is very dry, but cold.	
	28/1/17		The usual Divine Service Parades were held. The following F.G.C.M. Promulgation took place: No 53128. Pte. F.W. Y. Gasker, 3 months. F.P. No 1. + to pay value 14/9. + No H/03583 Pte. L. Wilson, fined £1. + awarded 2 months F.P. No 1. Weather good, very cold.	
	29/1/17		Day training has been carried on. The day has been Bathed & received pay. Enemy aircraft has been very active at night many Bombs were dropped in the vacinity but did no actual damage. Weather good.	
	30/1/17		The day received hot bath & change of clothing & new Clothchies [?] is in the course of enistment. Enemy aircraft have again been active many Bombs were dropped last night but no damage done. Weather good.	

2353 Wt. W2544/1454 700,000 5/15 D. D. & L. A.D.S.S. Forms/C. 2118.

WAR DIARY
or
INTELLIGENCE SUMMARY.

(Erase heading not required.)

Army Form C. 2118.

Place	Date	Hour	Summary of Events and Information	Remarks and references to Appendices
CHIPILLY	31/1/17		The Coy training has been carried on. Guns, Belts, ammunition & equipment have all been thoroughly cleaned, overhauled & repaired. The bathhouse has now been completed. Weather good, still very cold.	

In the field
1st Feb. 1917.

Mathieson Major.
Commanding 121 M.G. Coy.

Original Copy

Vol 9

Confidential

War Diary of

121 Machine Gun Company

From 1st February 1917 to 28th February 1917

Volume 8

Army Form C. 2118.

WAR DIARY
or
INTELLIGENCE SUMMARY.
(Erase heading not required.)

Instructions regarding War Diaries and Intelligence Summaries are contained in F. S. Regs., Part II and the Staff Manual respectively. Title pages will be prepared in manuscript.

Place	Date	Hour	Summary of Events and Information	Remarks and references to Appendices
CAMP.12. CHIPILLY.	1/2/17		The day training has been carried on. Lt. A.R. Mali returned from Hospital. Enemy aeroplanes were over & dropped several bombs but did no damage. Weather fair, very cold.	
	2/2/17		The day was spent in the throughly overhaul all the transport etc. Enemy aircraft were over & dropped several bombs, damage nil. Weather good, very cold.	
	3/2/17		The day training has been resumed. There has been a lot of sickness owing to the extremely cold weather. Weather good, very cold.	
	4/2/17		The O.C. Coy, Lt. A.M.R. Bain & 2 O.R's attended a demonstration of aeroplanes in connection with anti aircraft firing. The day carried on with day training. Weather good, very cold.	
	5/2/17		The day training has been carried on. Lt. L.H. Bretus & 1 O.R's proceeded on M.G. course at M.G. School at CAMIERS. Weather good, very cold.	

Army Form C. 2118.

WAR DIARY
or
INTELLIGENCE SUMMARY.
(Erase heading not required.)

Instructions regarding War Diaries and Intelligence Summaries are contained in F. S. Regs., Part II. and the Staff Manual respectively. Title pages will be prepared in manuscript.

Place	Date	Hour	Summary of Events and Information	Remarks and references to Appendices
CAMP. 12 CHIPILLY.	6/2/17		The finding of the G.G.C.M. in case of Dr. Wilson & Pvt. Gashy has been approved the sentences confirmed. The O.C. boy proceeded on leave to the U.K. The boy was paid. The boy training has been carried on. Weather good, very cold.	
	7/2/17		The Transport Section have now taken over Billets in the village of CHIPILLY. 30 O.R's were invest with IAR reinforcements from the Base. Weather good, very cold.	
	8/2/17		The O.C. 40 Div. Train inspected the Harness & sent in a very favourable report. No. Sgt. H. Orr has been transferred to the Base. The boy is carrying on with training. Weather good, very cold.	
	9/2/17		Orders have been received that the boy will move to camps No 111 on the 11th inst. The boy training is going on. Weather good, very cold.	
	10/2/17		2th A.Q.M.A. with 2 gun teams proceeded to BRAY on Anti-aircraft duties. Boy training carried on. Weather good, very cold.	

Army Form C. 2118.

WAR DIARY
or
INTELLIGENCE SUMMARY.
(Erase heading not required.)

Instructions regarding War Diaries and Intelligence Summaries are contained in F. S. Regs., Part II. and the Staff Manual respectively. Title pages will be prepared in manuscript.

Place	Date	Hour	Summary of Events and Information	Remarks and references to Appendices
CAMP 111 BRAY.	11/2/17		The Bty marched at 2.25 p.m. & arrived at Camp 111 at 5.25 p.m. taking over Billets. 2/Lt. S.J. Warn & No 33292 Gnr L. Elland returned from leave. 1 O.R. reinforcement reported from C.C.S. Weather good, very cold.	
	12/2/17		The Bty training was resumed. Gp Cpl P. Shilobrake proceeded on bombing course to FLEXICOURT. Weather cold, very frosty.	
	13/2/17		Bty training has been carried on. Lt D.G. Army Parker from the 23rd A.S. Bty. reported for duty as 2/i/c Command and No 64916 Dr. Gumming reported for duty from Base. Weather has broken, thaw has set in, very cold.	
	14/2/17		Lt Bain & Lt Parker proceeded to RANCOURT to reconnoitre positions for 16 guns to straightened line in cooperation with Artillery on the 15th inst. The Bty training has been carried on. Weather cold, windy but dry.	
	15/2/17		No 39041 Le Cpl P. Maher was tried by F.G.M. Sgr Lloyd proceeded on short Gas course at CAMP 21	

Army Form C. 2118.

WAR DIARY
or
INTELLIGENCE SUMMARY.
(Erase heading not required.)

Instructions regarding War Diaries and Intelligence Summaries are contained in F. S. Regs., Part II. and the Staff Manual respectively. Title pages will be prepared in manuscript.

Place	Date	Hour	Summary of Events and Information	Remarks and references to Appendices
CAMP III BRAY	15/2/17		The Coy left at 8.30 a.m. for RANCOURT, arriving at 2 p.m. all guns in position at 3 p.m. Harassing fire was carried out in co-operation with artillery until 4.20 p.m. Arrived back in camp at 9.30 p.m. Weather Wet.	
	16/2/17		Ground gun of 7.G.C.M. on Lt.64. O. Maker returned to rations + 3 months H.Q. N° 1. Two gun teams relieved 2 anti aircraft guns of 120 M.G. Coy at BRAY. The Coy overhauled guns + refilled belts. Weather thawing	
	17/2/17		Orders were received that this Coy will relieve 119 M.G. Coy on night of 22/23rd inst in RANCOURT Sector. The Coy Training has been carried on. Weather damp + foggy.	
	18/2/17		The usual Divine Service parades were attended. The Coy received Baths in BRAY. 8 lectures was delivered on Contact Patrols, 3 officers of this Coy attended. Weather damp + foggy.	

Army Form C. 2118.

WAR DIARY
or
INTELLIGENCE SUMMARY.
(Erase heading not required.)

Instructions regarding War Diaries and Intelligence Summaries are contained in F.S. Regs., Part II. and the Staff Manual respectively. Title pages will be prepared in manuscript.

Place	Date	Hour	Summary of Events and Information	Remarks and references to Appendices
CAMP.III. BRAY.	19/2/17		The transport was inspected. The Coy training was carried on. Weather Wet.	
LE FOREST	20/2/17		The Coy relieved 119th M.G. Coy's Guns n.e. 5.6.7 & 8 also 2 Anti Aircraft guns at LEFOREST. Remainder of the Coy carried on with training. Weather Wet.	
	21/2/17		One gun team proceeded to BRAY thus making one complete section at BRAY. G.O.R's reinforcements from BASE. Weather fair. The remainder of Coy took over from 119th M.G. Coy in the	
RANCOURT	22/2/17		RANCOURT sectn. The 119th Coy kept 4 teams on the Guthumedium Gun & the 2 teams on anti aircraft at LE FOREST. Relief completed 9.15 p.m. Weather very wet.	
	23/2/17		The Artillery has been very active in both orders. Work has proceeded very well. Cashalties Nil. Weather Wet.	
	24/2/17		The Artillery has again been very active on both sides. 2nd Lieutn. W. Watts ——— admitted to Hospital sick. Weather Good.	

WAR DIARY
or
INTELLIGENCE SUMMARY.

Army Form C. 2118.

Place	Date	Hour	Summary of Events and Information	Remarks and references to Appendices
RANCOURT	25/2/17		Lt. G. L. Rowe & 2 O.R's proceeded to CAMIERS for M.G. Service. Details from CAMIERS. 2 O.R's returned from M.G. School CAMIERS. Lt. A. G. Bain relieved Lt. E. Andrews. The Artillery on both sides has been very active. Casualties Nil. Weather good.	
	26/2/17		Lt. E. Andrews proceeded to MAUREPAS on an escort & has been placed under arrest in charge of 21st Middlesex Rgt to await trial by F.G.C.M. for Neglect of Duty on Trenches. The O.C. Coy returned from leave. The Artillery activity still continues on both sides. Casualties Nil. Weather Good.	
	27/2/17		The enemy aircraft have been very active. The Artillery activity still continues on both sides. Casualties Nil. The O.C. Coy accompanied the L.G.O.C. & Corps. M.G. Officer on a tour of inspection & reconnaissance of several new gun positions. Weather Good.	
	28/2/17		Two successful Raids were carried out by the Division on our left. Artillery very active on both sides. Casualties Nil. Weather good.	

Nathan Major
O.C. 124 M.G. Coy.

Original copy

Vol 10

Confidential

War Diary
of
121 Machine Gun Coy.
Machine Gun Corps

From 1st March 1917 to 31st March 1917.

Volume 9

WAR DIARY
or
INTELLIGENCE SUMMARY.
(Erase heading not required.)

Army Form C. 2118.

Place	Date	Hour	Summary of Events and Information	Remarks and references to Appendices
RANCOURT	1/3/17		The Artillery on both sides has been very active by day & night. No. 26682. Pte. C. Edmonds was seriously wounded. Work on Emplacements has progressed favourably. Weather Good.	
	2/3/17		Conditions remain much the same. Artillery on both sides has been very active day & night, otherwise things are very quiet. Work is progressing. Weather Good.	
	3/3/17		The Shelling is still very active. Our Artillery is undoubtedly superior. We certainly have the upperhand & bombarded enemy trenches, severely damaged his front line trench. Work still progressing. Weather fine.	
	4/3/17		Orders have been received that the 8th Divs will attack at 5:15 a.m. & take FRITZ & PALLAS Trenches. Our Artillery has been shelling enemy lines day & night very heavily. The 23rd, 24th, 25th & 120th Machine Gun Coys have been ordered to put up Barrage Fire, in co-operation with	

Army Form C. 2118.

WAR DIARY
or
INTELLIGENCE SUMMARY.
(Erase heading not required.)

Instructions regarding War Diaries and Intelligence Summaries are contained in F. S. Regs., Part II. and the Staff Manual respectively. Title pages will be prepared in manuscript.

Place	Date	Hour	Summary of Events and Information	Remarks and references to Appendices
RANCOURT	4/3/17		and Artillery. Weather Wet. Snow fall during the night.	
	5/3/17		The 8th Div. attacked at 5.15 a.m. aided by a very heavy Artillery & M.G. Barrage & gained their objective by 6 a.m. The enemy put up a very heavy Barrage & made several counter attacks, all of which failed. All new positions have been maintained. 200 Prisoners & 3 M.G.'s have been captured. Weather Wet.	
	6/3/17		Artillery on both sides has been very heavy on several occasions. Barrage fire has been carried out & further enemy counter-attacks repulsed. New positions have been consolidated. Weather fair.	
	7/3/17		This Coy was relieved by the 23rd & 24th M.G. Coys. There is much Artillery activity but the enemy have not been so active today. Weather fair.	
SUZANNE	8/3/17		The Coy arrived at Barrels 17 at about 3 a.m. I.O.R. from the Base reported for duty. Weather good, cold, windy	

WAR DIARY
or
INTELLIGENCE SUMMARY.

(Erase heading not required.)

Army Form C. 2118.

Place	Date	Hour	Summary of Events and Information	Remarks and references to Appendices
SUZANNE	9/3/17		The Coy has been overhauling guns + equipment. No 263484 L.Cpl. A. Shildrake returned from bookkeepers course. Weather good.	
	10/3/17		The Guns, Equipment + Ammunition are being thoroughly overhauled. The Coy had Bathm SUZANNE. Weather wet.	
	11/3/17		Coy attended a conference at Bde Hqr. The O.C. Coy attended a Conference at Bde Hqr. Weather wet. The usual Divine Services were attended. A miniature Range has been constructed. Weather good.	
	12/3/17		The following N.C.O.'s were tried by G.C.M. for neglect of duty in trenches. No 30743 Sgt. J. Lloyd & No 29026 L/Cpl S. Ash. The Coy training was carried on. L.C. Anderson was tried this morning by G.C.M. for neglect of duty in the trenches. Weather wet.	
	13/3/17		The Coy carried out firing on the range + all Belts used were refilled. Weather wet.	
CURLU	14/3/17		The following N.C.O. + men were tried at Camp 17 by G.C.M. No 29699 Sgt. J. Daly, No 29695 Pte. D. Moa, No 29027	

Army Form C. 2118.

WAR DIARY
or
INTELLIGENCE SUMMARY.
(Erase heading not required.)

Instructions regarding War Diaries and Intelligence Summaries are contained in F. S. Regs., Part II. and the Staff Manual respectively. Title pages will be prepared in manuscript.

Place	Date	Hour	Summary of Events and Information	Remarks and references to Appendices
CURLU	14/3/17		Ph. Bagly. E. The Coy marched at 2p.m. to P.C. CHAPEAU + took over Billets. Orders received that this Coy will relieve 119th M.G. Coy in CLERY Sector on the 16th inst. Weather good.	
	15/3/17		The O.C. Coy reconnoitred trenches in the CLERY Sector. Promulgation of G.R.O. re No. 29026 Dvr. J. Ash. Sentence Reduced to the Ranks + 3 months No. 21 H.Q. Weather good.	
CLERY	16/3/17		The Coy relieved the 119th M.G. Coy in the CLERY Sector. The enemy shelled the Road as the Coy was unpacking Limbers, fortunately all shells that actually hit the Road were Duds, otherwise we should have had many casualties. No. 68172 Pte. Mahany wounded by sniper. Enemy sent over Gas shells at 5p.m. otherwise quiet. Weather Good.	
	17/3/17		Our troops have been patrolling very actively. Enemy very quiet. Reinforcements 5 O.R's from Base. Promulgation of G.R.O. No. 24699 Sgt. J. Daly. Sentence Reduced to rank	

WAR DIARY or INTELLIGENCE SUMMARY

Place	Date	Hour	Summary of Events and Information	Remarks and references to Appendices
CLERY	17/3/17		A Cpl. & No 27698 Pte. O. Moran. Detained 1 days Pay. Orders desired that no troops must force way into enemy trenches before dawn. Weather Good.	
	18/3/17		Our troops entered enemy trenches & found them deserted. Patrols & outposts were at once pushed forward. Our front has been reported clear as far as Mt. St. Quentin & flank slopes. Cavalry Patrols have pushed forward. 2/Lt. Y.M. Hull has reported from the Base for duty. Lt. G. L. Rowe & 2 O.R's have returned from the M.G. School CAMIERS. 2 O.R's proceeded to CAMIERS to course at the M.G. School. 8 Guns have been pushed forward into the German Support line to cover TORTILLE VALLEY. Weather Good.	
PERRONNE	19/3/17		The enemy are still retiring along whole of our front. Our Patrols report that AIZECOURT - TINCOURT-LE-HAUT, BUSSU & PERRONNE are now clear of enemy. A new line of resistance has been taken up from HILL 75 in F20, MOUNT-ST-QUENTIN	

WAR DIARY
or
INTELLIGENCE SUMMARY
(Erase heading not required.)

Army Form C. 2118.

Place	Date	Hour	Summary of Events and Information	Remarks and references to Appendices
PERRONNE	19/3/17		to HAUT ALLAINES. We are at present keeping in touch with the 48th D in 3rd Corps. Our transport has just moved from FRISE BEND to near CLERY CEMETERY. Weather Wet.	
Mt ST QUENTIN	20/3/17		The 8 guns at present covering the TORTILLE VALLEY have been ordered to proceed to BOSSU. The other 8 guns are in position in our new line of resistance. Transport has now moved up to FEUILLACOURT. Weather Good.	
MOUNT-ST-QUENTIN	21/3/17		The O.C. has reconnoitred the new outpost line & 6 guns have been placed in position about 1 mile in front of BOSSU. The Transport arrived at FEUILLACOURT at 11 a.m. We have not seen any signs of the enemy, our cavalry patrols report having been in touch some miles ahead. Weather good.	
	22/3/17		The enemy have not been seen, everything is very quiet. Our cavalry report having been in touch, pursuit party of L.C.M. of 2 Lt. C. Andrews. Sentence, to be dismissed from	

WAR DIARY or INTELLIGENCE SUMMARY

Army Form C. 2118.

Place	Date	Hour	Summary of Events and Information	Remarks and references to Appendices
MOUNT-ST-QUENTIN.	22/3/17		His Majestys Service. Weather Good.	
	23/3/17		Still no signs of enemy, everything very quiet, Balloony report that patrols were shelled from TEMPLEUX-LA-FOSSE. 2/Lt. C. Anderson left for the Base in rank for U.K. under escort of 2/Lt C.H. SLIGHT of 21st Middlesex Regt. No.25711 Pte. O.H. Taylor sent to the Base, underage. Reinforcements. 1 O.R. from Base. Weather Good.	
	24/3/17		Orders received we are to be relieved by the 48th Divn on the 25/3/17. Enemy very quiet. Weather Good. Very cold.	
	25/3/17		The Bn has been relieved two have moved to a new Camp just outside of MI-SI-QUENTIN. Enemy very quiet. Several enemy aeroplanes have been over. Weather Good.	
	26/3/17		The Coy has been turned on to road making & work from 8 a.m. to 12 noon. 12.30 p.m. to 4.30 p.m. daily. Weather Wet	
	27/3/17		The Coy is on Road making all day. 14367 L/Cpl J Clarke & 27697 L/Cpl W. Flannaghan. were dispatched to the Base	

Army Form C. 2118.

WAR DIARY
or
INTELLIGENCE SUMMARY.
(Erase heading not required.)

Place	Date	Hour	Summary of Events and Information	Remarks and references to Appendices
MOUNT-ST- QUENTIN	27/3/17		en route for ENGLAND. Reinforcements I.O.R. from Base. Weather Wet.	
	28/3/17		Received orders to Place to Guns for such through Work. The Coy is still making Road. The weather has been very bad. One of d. trap position has been completed. Weather Wet.	
	29/3/17		Two anti aircraft positions have now been completed. Remainder of the Coy is still doing Road Work. Weather very bad.	
	30/3/17		Two more anti-aircraft positions have been completed. Improvements in Camp are progressing rapidly. The Coy is still on Road making. Weather very bad.	
	31/3/17		The O.C. & 2 Section Officers attended Conference & lectured down at Bde Hdqrs. The Coy are still working on the Roads. Weather has been very bad.	

In the Field.
31/3/17

J Mathisen Major.
OC 121 A.T. Coy.

To Ayr
101st Inf Brigade

No. 121
MACHINE GUN
COMPANY.
No. 3/B
Date 1-5-17

Enclosed please find War diary for the month of April 1917.

P Mathison Major
OC 121 M.G. Coy

3/5/17

Original Copy.

Vol XI

Confidential

War Diary

of

121 Machine Gun Company

Machine Gun Corps.

from :- 1st April 1917.   to :- 30th April 1917.

Volume 10

Army Form C. 2118.

WAR DIARY
or
INTELLIGENCE SUMMARY.
(Erase heading not required.)

Place	Date	Hour	Summary of Events and Information	Remarks and references to Appendices
MOUNT ST. QUENTIN	1/4/17		The Coy is still on Road work. The 2nd in command with 2 section Officers attended Tactical Exercise at Bois Fludges. Orders have been received that this Coy takes over part of the line on 30th April	Weather Wet.
	2/4/17		The Coy is still on Road work. Orders were received at 9 p.m. to reconnoitre the old Line of Resistance which had been occupied by the XV Corps, i.e. NURLU, LIERMONT. Both inclusive to be ready to occupy same at a moments notice either by day or night. Five enemy aeroplanes were over the camp at 7.30 a.m.	Weather Wet.
	3/4/17		The Coy was given today to overhaul & clean kit, guns & equipment. One mule was destroyed by order of the Vet Surgeon. The men have received an issue of clean clothes.	Weather Wet.
	4/4/17		The Coy has been on Road work. One mule had to be destroyed owing to having leg broken by a kick from heavy draught horse. The weather continues to be very wet & stormy.	
	5/4/17		Orders received that the Coy will take over part of the line in front of FINS. No. 1 Sec. has been attached to 13th Yorks. No. 2 Sec. attached to the 21st Middlesex & moved to ETRICOURT the remainder of the Coy move to EQUANCOURT on 6/4/17	Weather Wet.

Army Form C. 2118.

WAR DIARY
or
INTELLIGENCE SUMMARY.
(Erase heading not required.)

Place	Date	Hour	Summary of Events and Information	Remarks and references to Appendices
EQUANCOURT	6/4/17		The Boy moved 9 a.m. arrived at Billets 1/p.m. The O.C. Boy has reconnoitred the sector. The Boy took over from Nos 25 & 59 M.G. Coys relief complete 11 p.m. Weather Wet.	
	7/4/17		Orders received that O.C. 1st Bde gp & 12th Div. will move to FINS tomorrow. The O.C. & 2nd i/c reconnoitred positions for 4 guns in the line. No 44456 Pte B. Instead, wounded. Shell Shock. Weather Wet.	
FINS.	8/4/17		Billets were taken over at 10 a.m. 4 & 2 guns have been mounted for Anti-aircraft work in guns & 2 guns have been placed in reserve at DESSART WOOD. The O.C. reconnoitred for other 4 gun positions. No 5699 Pte H Pollard, killed by shell fire, 2 mules were killed by shell fire. Reinforcements 3 O.Rs from BASE. Weather Wet.	
	9/4/17		The Bde made a small advance taking some high ground, casualties were 61 O.Rs killed & wounded (all 21st Middlesex Regt). Our M.G's fired 7000 rds & dispersed several parties. Casualties 2 O.Rs wounded. Leave Lt. A.M.R. Bain to U.K. from 20th to 20 inst. Weather Very Wet.	(10th to 20th)
	10/4/17		We now have 16 guns in the line. The 119th Boy has sent up 2 guns for Anti-aircraft duties at FINS. The usual shelling has been going on. Enemy very quiet. Weather Wet.	

WAR DIARY or INTELLIGENCE SUMMARY

Army Form C. 2118.

Place	Date	Hour	Summary of Events and Information	Remarks and references to Appendices
FINS.	11/4/17		Orders received that 24th M.G. Coy will take over the 6 guns on the right sector tonight. Lt. G.L. Stockley admitted to Hospital sick. Reinforcements 2/Lt. J.E. Ellis & 2/Lt. T. Thorpe reported for duty from the Base.	
	12/4/17		The 8th Div is on our Right attacked & captured GOUZEACOURT & GAUCHE WOOD & have consolidated. We have again taken over the 6 guns from the 24th M.G. Coy. Enemy very quiet. Weather wet.	
	13/4/17		The enemy have been very quiet. 2nd Lt. T.E. ELLIS admitted to hospital sick. Two new positions are being made at Q.23. central (Outpost line.) The usual shelling has been going on. The O.C. has reconnoitred the front with a view to pushing guns forward when the Boche advances. Weather wet.	
	14/4/17		The usual shelling has been going on. Enemy very quiet. Orders received that the 120 M.G. Coy will take over 10 guns in the line of resistance. Work is proceeding rapidly. Weather very unsettled & wet.	
	15/4/17		The 120th M.G Coy have relieved 10 guns which have returned	

Army Form C. 2118.

WAR DIARY
or
INTELLIGENCE SUMMARY.
(Erase heading not required.)

Instructions regarding War Diaries and Intelligence Summaries are contained in F. S. Regs., Part II. and the Staff Manual respectively. Title pages will be prepared in manuscript.

Place	Date	Hour	Summary of Events and Information	Remarks and references to Appendices
FINS	15/4/17		No Billets. The 2 nos emplacements have been employed. Work on Billets is progressing rapidly. Weather very unsettled. Snow & Rain.	
	16/4/17		The 10 Gun teams have been cleaning guns & equipments, working in Billets & drilling. A German aeroplane brought down one of our observation balloons. The enemy have been very quiet. Weather very Wet.	
	17/4/17		We have mounted 2 guns for Anti aircraft work & the other 8 Guns & teams have been sent back to ETRICOURT. The remainder of the Coy will be relieved on the 18 & 19th by the 120th M.G. Coy. Weather very unsettled. Enemy very quiet. The 120th M.G. Coy relieved the 6 guns in the Left flank. The Coy Head Qrs with 2 sections moved to ETRICOURT.	
ETRICOURT	18/4/17		to Billets in ETRICOURT arriving about 11.30 p.m. Weather fair. The Coy has been carrying on with training, Cleaning & Overhauling, guns & equipment. Lt. G.L. Rowe proceeded on leave to the U.K. No 29086 Pte W. Shegar proceeded to the Base for transfer to the Rly. R.E. & has been struck off strength. No 29051.	
	19/4/17			

WAR DIARY
or
INTELLIGENCE SUMMARY.

Army Form C. 2118.

Place	Date	Hour	Summary of Events and Information	Remarks and references to Appendices
ETRICOURT	19/4/17		Coy. 2. M. Sgt. M. Broderick left for on promotion to C.S.M. & transfer to 99 M.G. Coy. No 23519 Coy 2. M. Sgt. H. Thurgill has been transferred from 150 M.G. Coy & has been taken on the strength of this Coy. Weather fair.	
	20/4/17		The Coy has been carrying on with training. A short 30 yds range has been constructed. The O.C. attended a conference at Bde Headqrs. The Coy has drawn & received clean clothing. Weather Good.	
	21/4/17		The Coy has been firing on the Range & Type firing was carried out in the evening. The O.C. & 2/Lts attended a Tactical Exercise with the Bde Gen. Weather Good.	
	22/4/17		The usual Divine Service was attended. The O.C. with remainder of Officers attended a Tactical Exercise with the Bde General & the Coy's M.G. Officers. Weather fine.	
	23/4/17		The Coy has been cleaning Belts, S.A.A. & Limbers. Night firing was carried out by Nos 1 & 2 Sections	

WAR DIARY or INTELLIGENCE SUMMARY

Army Form C. 2118.

Place	Date	Hour	Summary of Events and Information	Remarks and references to Appendices
ETRICOURT	23/4/17		No 3 & 4 Sections were ordered to take over 8 gun positions from 120 M.G. Coy. Weather fine.	
FINS	24/4/17		The remainder of the Coy have been cleaning belts & S.A.A. Orders were received to stand tos at 12 noon. The Coy Headqrs with No 1 & 2 Sections moved to FINS & the 8 guns took over Reserve positions from 120 M.G. Coy. Weather fine.	
	25/4/17		The enemy were very quiet. The M.O. & 2/offr reconnoitred the line & visited all gun teams. Weather fine.	
	26/4/17		The Coy Head qrs moved to the Sunken Rd at Q.27.c.8.9. Enemy have been shelling BEAUCAMP & VILLIERS PLOUICH. Our artillery has been very active. Reinforcements, 3 O.R's from Base have been taken on the strength. Weather fine. No 25690 Pte W Jarvis slightly wounded.	
	27/4/17		Enemy artillery has been very active. No 44980 Pte W Noonan slightly wounded. No 44980 Pte W Noonan slightly wounded. Our Guns have been working. Weather fair.	

Army Form C. 2118.

WAR DIARY
or
INTELLIGENCE SUMMARY.
(Erase heading not required.)

Instructions regarding War Diaries and Intelligence Summaries are contained in F. S. Regs., Part II. and the Staff Manual respectively. Title pages will be prepared in manuscript.

Place	Date	Hour	Summary of Events and Information	Remarks and references to Appendices
DESSART WOOD (W.1.6.7.0.)	28/4/17		The Coy Headqrs have moved back to Dessart Wood (@ W.1.6.7.0) The No 20 M.G. Coy have taken over 8 position's in the New Reserve Line & our guns have been withdrawn from positions. No 1 Sect is now at GOUZEACOURT WOOD No 2 Section is at Sunken Rd. Q 27. c.8.0. - No 29031. Pk. C. Goodfellow + No 29005. Pk. E. Lestrange proceeded to CAMIERS for M.G. course. Weather Very fine.	
	29/4/17		The enemy Artillery has been very active on trenches at Q 18.d. (Sheet Reg. France. 57°. S.E. Edit. 3.A.) Orders were received that the 8 guns in reserve will relieve 119 M G Coy on night April 30/1 May. Weather fine. 2nd Lt. J.Q. Hale proceeded on leave to U.K.	
	30/4/17		Enemy Artillery + Enemy Stokes Mortars have been very active. 2nd Lt S. A WANN has been promoted Lt to date from 23/4/17. No 1 + 2 Sections relieved No 119 M.G. Coy. Weather fine. In the Field 30/4/17 Mathew in Maj 19 Apl 1917 O/C. 121 M. G. Coy.	

No. 121
MACHINE GUN
COMPANY
F.5.
1-6-17

To
Headquarters
121 Infy Brigade

Herewith please find War Diary for the month of May 1917.

P Mathison Major
Commanding 121 Machine Gun Coy.

1/6/17

Confidential

Original | copy

Vol 12

War Diary
of
121 Machine Gun Coy.
Machine Gun Corps

From :— 1st May 1917   To :— 31st May 1917

Volume No 12.

WAR DIARY
or
INTELLIGENCE SUMMARY.
(Erase heading not required.)

Army Form C. 2118.

Place	Date	Hour	Summary of Events and Information	Remarks and references to Appendices
DESSART WOOD.	1/5/17		Map Refce. 57ª S.E. Nos 1 & 2 Sects have taken over 8 gun positions from 119th M.G. Coy in the LA VACQUERIE. Reinforcements. 3 O.R.'s from Base. Leave. No 30070 Pte. Yeaton returned. Enemy artillery very active at night on R.19 central. Weather very fine.	
	2/5/17		Nos 3 & 4 Sects were relieved from VILLIERS PLUICH Sector by the 120 M.G. Coy & are Billetted in GOUZEACOURT WOOD. Casualties. 3 O.R. wounded. Leave. W.O. L. Parr returned. Shrapnel shelling very active. Our artillery has been very active on enemy work the. Weather very fine.	
	3/5/17		Orders received that positions for 24 guns had to be reconnoitred with a view to putting up an M.G. Barrage for an operation to take place in a few days. O.C. & 2i/c reconnoitred the sector & selected sites for groups of guns. Enemy artillery very active during the night & gas alarm was given but nothing developed. Casualties 1 O.R. killed & 1 wounded. Weather very fine.	

Army Form C. 2118.

WAR DIARY
or
INTELLIGENCE SUMMARY.
(Erase heading not required.)

Instructions regarding War Diaries and Intelligence Summaries are contained in F.S. Regs., Part II. and the Staff Manual respectively. Title pages will be prepared in manuscript.

Place	Date	Hour	Summary of Events and Information	Remarks and references to Appendices
DESSART WOOD	4/5/17		At 4.45 a.m. our artillery put up a Practice Barrage for 20 minutes. Enemy retaliated on our front trenches. Orders received that a Raid would be carried out by the 8th Div with 40th Div on the night 5/6 May on LA VACQUERIE. The 120 M.G. Coy has been placed under orders of G.O.C. 121 Infantry Bde & attached to my Coy. The Lectern Officers from 120 M.G. Coy with Nos. 3 & 4 Sections of 121 M.G. Coy Lewis Guns reconnoitred & laid out night lines for their Guns to do a Barrage fire on night of 5/6 May 1917. Weather very fine.	Map T.S. to Bde Orders Coy Orders Report Summary
	5/5/17		Operation Orders were received. The 24 Guns were in position by 10.45 p.m. & opened fire as per time table. Detailed Report with copies, time table & map attached. No. 1 Sect in the trenches had a gun knocked out. Casualties 2 O.Rs. killed, 2 wounded. Tens Nos. 9626 to 9649 No. 9641 sent to Abl. U.K. from 5/5/17 to 15/5/17. Weather very fine.	Indirect fire Sketch Time table

WAR DIARY or INTELLIGENCE SUMMARY

Army Form C. 2118.

Place	Date	Hour	Summary of Events and Information	Remarks and references to Appendices
DESSART WOOD	6/5/17		Enemy very quiet. The Operations last night were very successful. Infantry Report state that our Barrage was very effective and every was satisfactory. The 121 Infantry Bde took 5 prisoners. No 10260 Sgt. H. Williams left for UK to take up a commission. Has been sent off strength. Weather very fine.	
	7/5/17		Orders received that Bde. would readjust its front. The 119th M.G. Coy relieved no 2 right guns & took over from the 120 M.G. Coy their 2 right guns. 2/Lt Y.P. Humphries to Hospital sick. Lt. O.J. Shekby evacuated to U.K. sick. Lt. A.R. Bain slightly wounded by shell fire, at duty. Weather very fine.	
	8/5/17		The enemy are very quiet. There are no 8 guns in the Line & 8 guns in Reserve at GOUZEACOURT WOOD. The O.C. reconnoitred Corps Line with G.S.O. 1 for H gun positions. Weather very wet.	
	9/5/17		The O.C. has issued orders to reconnoitre ground with a view to Mogany gun's in this sector. One of our	

WAR DIARY
or
INTELLIGENCE SUMMARY.

Army Form C. 2118.

(Erase heading not required.)

Place	Date	Hour	Summary of Events and Information	Remarks and references to Appendices
DESSART WOOD	9/5/17		aeroplanes brought down by enemy plane about V.6.b. Central Map Ref 57.c S.E. Enemy has been very quiet. Leave. No 30747/3 Sgt Lloyd. J. on leave to the U.K. 10/5/17. Weather fine.	
	10/5/17		The O.C. & 2/Lt reconnoitred the line for positions for H guns for re adjustment of Bde area. The weather has been very fine. The enemy planes brought down one of our planes about R.14.C.00. The enemy have been very quiet. Our aeroplanes made a raid on all enemy Observation Balloons on the 4th Army Front at 3.15.p.m. Weather very fine.	
	11/5/17		Orders have been received that on the night of the 13/14 this Bay will be relieved by the 60th H.S. Bay & later on of the night of the 14/15. this Bay will relieve the 125 H.S. By in the VILLIERS GUSLAIN. The O.C. & 2/Lt reconnoitred the new sector. Orders received that new emplacements have to be made in present sector & H guns moved from present positions &	

WAR DIARY or INTELLIGENCE SUMMARY

Army Form C. 2118.

Place	Date	Hour	Summary of Events and Information	Remarks and references to Appendices
DESSART WOOD	11/5/17		To occupy the new area.	
	12/5/17		Reinforcements. 7 O.R's from Base. Work was commenced at 9p.m. The enemy have been very quiet. Weather very fine. The 4 new Emplacements have been completed & occupied. Leave. No 6503 Pte. Gossery returned from leave. Weather fine.	
HEUDECOURT	13/5/17		The Coy was relieved by the 65th M.G. Coy. & proceeded to Billets in new area, arriving at 12 p.m. midnight. Relief complete at 12.45.a.m. Leave. 2/Lt. A.G. Nole returned from U.K. Weather fine.	
VILLERS-GUISLAINS	14/5/17		The Coy left HEUDECOURT at 8 p.m. & proceeded to VILLERS GUISLAINS to relieve 25th M.G. Coy. Relief complete by 11.30 p.m. Leave. Lt. J.S. Amery Parkers proceeded to the U.K. 15.% 25/5/17. Courses No 29093 Sgt. @ Hugh on G.O.C. course. Very heavy thunder rain storm at 2.30 a.m. Weather fair.	
	15/5/17		The new sector is very quiet. Enemy aircraft active. The Front line guns have to be re-organised. The whole of this area is under observation & movement is very restricted.	

Army Form C. 2118.

WAR DIARY
or
INTELLIGENCE SUMMARY.
(Erase heading not required.)

Place	Date	Hour	Summary of Events and Information	Remarks and references to Appendices
VILLERS GUISLAINS	15/5/17 16/5/17		Casualties Nil. Weather very fine. Enemy very quiet. 4 Guns carried out Night firing on NOBLE VILLE. An enemy aeroplane brought down by our aircraft near GOUZEACOURT. Losses No 29011 Sgt M. McCarthy in Physical Training & Bayonet fighting. Weather fine.	
	17/5/17		Enemy very quiet. 8 Guns in Front line system have to be moved into new positions before Daylight 18/5/17. The O.C. toy reconnoitred 8 new positions for these guns. Losses Rev. Q.Rsm to U.K. 17/5/17 to 27/5/17. Losses No 29093 Sgr R Skeogh returned from Gas Course. Weather fine.	
	18/5/17		Enemy very quiet. The 8 Guns in the Front line system have been moved into the newly constructed positions. 4 Guns carried out Night firing on the village of HONNECOURT. Weather fine.	

WAR DIARY
or
INTELLIGENCE SUMMARY

Army Form C. 2118.

Place	Date	Hour	Summary of Events and Information	Remarks and references to Appendices
VILLERS GUISLIANS	19/5/17		One section (4 Guns) this taken our positions in the BROWN & BOYAU Lines. One section (4 Guns) have taken over positions in the GREEN & Intermediate Lines. Bde Conference was held at Hdqrs 20th Batt Middx Regt. The enemy have been very quiet. Weather fine.	
	20/5/17		The 8 Guns in the Hoxxx Line system were relieved by the 4 Guns from Brown Line & 4 Guns in Green Line. 3 Guns were moved to new positions & dug in during the night. 2 Guns were detailed to engage enemy M.G's that might fire from about X.11.b.7.5. Leave No.9626 Le Edp. M. Neal returned from U.K. & No. 27690 Sgt. E. Brennan proceeded to U.K. from 20/5/17 to 30th/5/17. 20 hours.— No.25696. Pvt. W. F. Davis to CAMIERS on M.G. course. No.23250. A/Cpl. B. Shad. to 4th Army Signal School. No.29031. Pvt. P. Goodfellow returned from M.G. School. CAMIERS No.29005. Pvt. E. Le Strange returned from M.G. School CAMIERS Weather fine.	

WAR DIARY or INTELLIGENCE SUMMARY

Army Form C. 2118.

Place	Date	Hour	Summary of Events and Information	Remarks and references to Appendices
VILLERS-GUISLAINS	21/5/17		Orders have been received that this Coy will be relieved on the nights 22/5/17 / 23/5/17 / 24/5/17 by the 106th M.G. Coy & that we shall then proceed to DESSART WOOD & relieve the 126 M.G. Coy in the VILLERS PLUICH sector. On the night of the 24/25/5/17.	
	22/5/17		The 106th M.G. Coy relieved No 1 & 2 Section in Guns Emp. Indirect fire with 4 Guns was carried out on HONNECOURT WOOD. No 1 & 2 Sects took over Billets in HEUDECOURT. Weather Fine.	
DESSART WOOD	23/5/17		The 106 M.G. Coy relieved No 3 & 4 Sects from the Bovril & Green Lines. The Coy is now Billeted in DESSART WOOD. No 29011. Sgt. Mahoney A. returned from a Physical Training course. Weather fine.	
	24/5/17		The Coy has been bathed & received clean clothes. The Coy relieved & took over 6 guns from the 125 A.G. Coy in fullz Church sector. Relief complete 11.45 p.m. Weather fine	

WAR DIARY
or
INTELLIGENCE SUMMARY.

Army Form C. 2118.

Place	Date	Hour	Summary of Events and Information	Remarks and references to Appendices
DESSART WOOD.	25/5/17		The Coy has taken over 3 Gun Emplts. from the 119 M.G. Coy. Indirect fire was carried out on PINE COPSE with 4 guns (Expend 12000 Rds S.A.A.) The enemy shelled DESSART WOOD & vicinity with 12 H.E. 5.9 shells & 29 5.16 Ph. & S. shells slightly wounded. O.C. Coy has been mentioned in Dispatches of todays date. Leave. No 30743 Sgt J. Hogarth---- Weather fine	
	26/5/17		The enemy are very quiet. Indirect fire with 6 Guns has been carried out on GOODMAN FARM & VICINITY. Weather fine.	
	27/5/17		The enemy are very quiet. We have placed another gun in the line. The enemy Copper Barrage in case of attack Indirect fire has been carried out on Rds, Cross Rds, & Farms at P.8.6. Ref Map 57° S.E.2. Weather fine.	
	28/5/17		The enemy have been very quiet. Indirect fire has been carried out on Rly & Rds in P.8.a. with 6 Guns. (16,000 rds) Leave. Lt. J. S. Young Parkes returned from U.K. Emplacements in Front Line are being improved. Weather fine	

Army Form C. 2118.

WAR DIARY
or
INTELLIGENCE SUMMARY.
(Erase heading not required.)

Instructions regarding War Diaries and Intelligence Summaries are contained in F. S. Regs., Part II. and the Staff Manual respectively. Title pages will be prepared in manuscript.

Place	Date	Hour	Summary of Events and Information	Remarks and references to Appendices
DESSART WOOD	29/5/17		The enemy are very very quiet. Indirect fire has been carried out on Jäger Lt R.15. central on enemy trench system. Gas Lt. S.A. Warn provided to U.K. No 29576 Ch. A.I. Anstr provided to U.K. Weather fine.	
	30/5/17		The enemy are very quiet. Our guns have again engaged targets at GOODMAN FARM + vicinity with Indirect fire. 6 Guns (18,000 rds SAA.) Work on Emplacements is proceeding rapidly. Weather fine.	
	31/5/17		The enemy are very quiet. Indirect fire has been carried out with 6 guns on Targets at R.8.a Roads + tram Rds. Work on emplacements is getting on very well & new alternative emplacement has been completed. Weather fine.	

In the Field
31/5/17

Mathesin Major
O.C. 121 M.G. Coy.

Army Form C. 2118.

WAR DIARY
or
INTELLIGENCE SUMMARY.
(Erase heading not required.)

Place	Date	Hour	Summary of Events and Information	Remarks and references to Appendices
			Summary.	
			Casualties.	
			Killed Wounded Admitted to Hospital & Evacuated	
			Officers Nil 1 1	
			W.C.O's Nil 2 2	
			O.Rs. 3 6 10	
			Total 25 All Ranks	
			Reinforcements	
			Officers Nil	
			N.C.O's Nil	
			O.Rs 13	
			Total 13 Other Ranks	
			Indirect Fire	
			Number of Guns in action 60 (Not counting guns from any other	
			Expenditure of S.A.A. 172,000. Company)	
			Number of Targets Engaged 17	
			Mathieson Major	
31/5/17			O.C. 121 M.G. Coy.	

OPERATION ORDERS
BY MAJOR P. MATHISEN.
O.C. 121 MACHINE GUN COMPANY
5-5-17.

MAP REFER. 57a S.E. 1/10000

1. The 121st Infantry Brigade on the night of the 5/6 May will raid the Enemy lines about LA VACQUERIE For this operation the 120th Machine Gun Company is attached to the 121st Infantry Brigade.

2. The 120th Machine Gun Company with numbers 3 & 4 Sections. No. 121st Machine Gun Company will put a Barrage around the objective.

3. Number 1 Section (2nd Lt. T. Thorp) for purposes of this operation will be attached to the 12th Battalion Suffolk Regiment.

4. Number 2 Section will remain in its present position in the line.

5. Advanced Company Headquarters will be at FIFTEEN RAVINE under Lt. A.J. Amery Parkes the O.C. 121st Machine Gun Company will be at advanced Brigade Headquarters at Q 29. a 9.5.

6. To simplify matters the Guns will be worked in groups No. 1 to 7.

7.
No. 1 Group 2 Guns   2nd Lt. H. Hull.
No. 2 Group 2 Guns   Lt. G. L. Rowe.
No. 3 Group 4 Guns   Lt. Rom
No. 4 Group 4 Guns   2nd Lt. Page.
No. 5 Group 4 Guns   2nd Lt. Scott
No. 6 Group 4 Guns   2nd Lt. Kennet
No. 7 Group 4 Guns   2nd Lt. Macfarlane

1.

8. The Guns of all Groups to be in position by 10-30 P.M. and to open fire as per attached time table.

9. Limbers with S.A.A. Guns, Equipment etc. to leave GOUZECOURT WOOD at 8 P.M and proceed to FIFTEEN RAVINE.

10. Carrying party of 100 men will be at FIFTEEN RAVINE by 9 P.M.

11. Guns and teams etc. will be withdrawn at 3-15 A.M. to FIFTEEN RAVINE.

12. Transport will be at FIFTEEN RAVINE by 3-30 A.M. and all Guns Equipment teams etc. will move to GOUZECOURT WOOD quickly as possible.

13. The O.C. Company will be in direct telephone communication with all Groups and a system of runners will be established through the Advanced Company Headquarters should the telephone break down.

14. Lt. Bain, 2nd Lt. Hull, Lt. Ardale and Lt. Scott will be at Group positions by dusk and lay out night lines, leaving their sub-section Officers to bring on their Sections.

15. All Section Officers will make necessary arrangements and ensure that the following points are attended to:-
   1. Screens for hiding Gun flash.
   2. 1 Petrol can Water per Gun.
   3. All oil Cans to be filled and taken on Gun position.
   4. Watches synchronised.
   5. Illuminated Night Firing Boxes to be used.
   6. Each Gun to have not less than 9,500 rounds S.A.A.
   7. Guns to be frequently checked by Clinometer or Sidney Level.

8. Depression Stops to be used, or if not fitted to Tripods, barriers to be put up.

9. Arrangements to be made to change round Gun numbers.

10. Condenser Bags and Tubes to be fitted.

16. <u>Reports.</u> Group Officers will report to the Advanced Company Headquarters by runner, and the O.C. Company by Telephone when all guns are in position. A Report of Operations to be rendered at Company Headquarters by 6 A.M. A detailed report will be called for later.

4/5/17

P. Mathison. Major.
O.C. 121 M.G. Coy.

Report on Operations

on the night of 5th/6th May 1917

— at —

LA VACQUERIE

P. Mathison, Major
O.C. 121 MACHINE GUN COMPANY
121 INFANTRY BRIGADE
IN THE FIELD

DATE 9th May 1917

MAP. REFER: I.S. 54/10000   GENERAL REMARKS.

SUBJECT	REMARKS	DIFFICULTIES ENCOUNTERED ETC:-
Transportation:- Transport, Traffic, Carrying Party	6 limbers were sent to be enough for Guns & 8 hrs Ammunition were loaded which was the fact in Bapaume. BOIZEAUCOURT WOOD at 8 P.M. & Left at 1 A.M. to FIFTEEN RAVINE where Ammn was unloaded & back to BOIZEAUCOURT WOOD & be. Congestion of traffic caused delay on the bridge & on Peronne - Rois. Carrying party of 100 men given & party used for carrying Kit, Canvas, Ammunition, up in fairly good time.	Carrying party facilitated matters, as the Carrying party team were used once the bridge could have been done in journey.
Ammunition:- Supply, Quantity used	12 lulls & 2 tins GPO, in all 9500 rounds, per gun were carried up. Average Ammunition used per gun was about 5000 rounds.	Cordite belts were Ammunition which had been caused from stood to stood from Ammn trenches. Note "STOPPAGES"
Laying Guns:- Method of Laying Night Lines, Laying Guns, Depression Stops, Clutching Guns, Allowances for wear of day, Instruments used, Hiding Gun Flash	Gun positions were reconnoitred the previous evening. Night lines were found by means of Compass & Pole. Guns laid by Abney Level & Clinometer. Elevation stops were not used as guns have been in the trenches more than once a week and we have not had occasion to fit them. Gun were checked periodically by Abney Level & Night Lines but as lack of ... Quite effective. No stoppages occurred in Ammo. ABNEY LEVEL, PRISMATIC COMPASS, CLINOMETERS, ELEVATING DIALS by No 5 N.B. 15 yd minute ... Gun flashes were not - hire have always proved to be sufficient trackmarks of camouflaging the posts.	In the laying of Guns the Abney Level worked to repel particular. Considerable drainage of water because particular care in aiming had to be taken. Considerable practice & some little time in laying before Scnarrs delay by night firing trades.
Control:- Clearing rate of fire, Guns, Times	NCO's of each gun were responsible for these. Ammo was checked at each ... as guns in use as by No 1 themselves. Control largely depended on nature of targets. An once came under Red & Frendes were used & control was by means of whistle.	Carriers of Ammn were not be awkward system during of the war but in Rise cases each NCO could give a corn/... of fire. Tales & recces were made for this to stopped fire.
Stoppages:- Nature of Stoppages, Stoppages, Water and Oil Supply	Practically all stoppages were of No 3 Type and occurred at Nos I and II brechen. These were hammered and were invaluable. Oiled down operations. 1 - Misspits. 1 - Slack Bore. Cartridges owned one belt instead of water under funnel & bellastrelle. & wanting & Prussian mind of ... howevery regularly ... The amount of deflogged in friendly to Hamburg translates & good far 15 hrs., passed & to Guide Sheepshot.	Spewings was made with lemon. Belts and hot bread with water, except overnight. South Stockers and quits & 400 of ammunition. Knobs was freed on this & Seni on ... No 20 (Deg) were made for Kensaw, Hamm, balls, cough & h great delay as more water ... powders & ...
Communication:- Telephone, Runners, Repeats	Telephone Communication was satisfactory between position & runners. Got dep 0 RMCH to have ... ordered to a most most remand to action, & they stoped 300 yards apart. A man in action to get the bullets No 1 instructs ... Runners were posted at CSRs HQrs, FIFTEEN RAVINE. Reports were delayed & control not so direct as the Artillery was fully aware the nature of Ammo used, & such fire.	Observation that telephonic communication was satisfactory but cost fairly & instrumes ... animositically the failing unless to Ballistrare cable between those 2 sub-types have ... . So was... can and what No most or such ... for action that are of use by peer fire. Considerable difficulty was to analyse.

Report on Operations
at
LA VACQUERIE
on
5th 6th May 1917

121 Machine Gun Company

Map Reference T.S. 60 Attached
Scheme   see Bde orders attached
Results   very satisfactory & successful so far as present known

Preliminary Arrangements

On the night of the 3/4 May 1917 the OC Coy with 2/i/c carried out a preliminary reconnaissance & orders were issued to the Section Officers concerned to reconnoitre certain areas & select the actual gun positions. This was carried out on the night of 4th/5th May 1917 & positions selected as per attached map

It was found that not less than 6 fighting limbers & 3 SAA limbers could be used to transport the 24 guns SAA etc to the advanced Coy Hdqrs at FIFTEEN RAVINE which was the nearest point to the gun positions that Transport could be taken

It was rather disappointing that the actual dumping ground was so far from gun positions for a lot of time was lost owing to distance to be covered by Carrying Party

The Carrying Party of 100 men proved scarcely sufficient to cope with the ammunition supply and in some cases they had to make 2 and 3 trips back and forward. Owing to the enemy Barrage they were held up during the second trip, the result was that in some cases guns had to slow down, which interfered with the Rates of Fire (see Time Table attached).

The Distance was from 600 yds to 1650 yds

Had there been any casualties in the Carrying Party the firing would have been very seriously interfered with.

Owing to the shortness of time definite orders not being issued until morning of the 5th. it was not possible to make Dumps near positions as they were <u>All</u> under observation.

FIFTEEN RAVINE being the only possible position in the forward area for a base of Operations for all troops engaged there was a certain amount of congestion which to some extent caused a certain amount of delay.

The ground is very hilly & was not very suitable for Machine Guns on Indirect Covering Fire.

The Infantry were advancing from our Front Line at about R 14 b 9.5 to R 14 d 0.4 & making a Raid on Trenches NE of LA VACQUERIE & on the village itself commencing at 11 pm & remaining in the captured positions until 1 AM at which time they were to withdraw

<u>Battle Action</u>

My 24 guns were used as a Covering & Flanking Barrage & assisted by the Machine Gun Corps of the 8th. Div: firing over their own area.

The guns averaged 5000 rds each, a total of 116000 rds of SAA were expended during the operation by my 24 guns.

The fire employed was in all cases Overhead, Indirect, Fixed Barrage Fire from ranges of 1900 to 2400 yds

3

Conclusions.

The Tactical results of this was that the Left Front & an open Flank was effectively covered.

The Infantry did not like advancing under the cones of fire but there were no complaints of any kind, they admitted they were glad to have this support

Notes :-

I do not believe it advisable to depend on SAA Dumps in the line for supply, it is safest to draw from the Coy Supply & take the necessary amount with the guns, replacing this from D.A.C before the Operation & so ensure Coy Reserve being intact.

An extra 1000 rds SAA was taken to the gun position for each gun, in case of a heavy counter attack & guns had to remain in positions & do heavy firing.

No emplacements were made owing to the danger of giving positions away, or raising suspicion of impending operations

In the field
9. 5. 1917

P. Mathisen. Major
O.C 121. M.G. Coy.

INDIRECT OVERHEAD FIRE.

No. 121 M.G. Coy. No. 3 & 4 Section. S Date 5/6 May 1917 Map used 57 C. S.E. 1:10,000 Officer i/c Firing Lt. G. L. ROWE

Gun No.	Target	ELEVATION						CLEARANCE OVER OWN TROOPS.					DIRECTION.	Time of firing	No. of rounds fired	Checked by	REMARKS. General.
		Range to Target in Yards	Contours in Yards Gun A	Contours in Yards Target	V.I. in Yards	Q.E. in Minutes Table 3(A) or 3(B)	Range for Q.E. in Yards Table 1, Col. 2	Contour of own troops in Yards B	Range to own troops in Yards	Traj. Height in Yards Table 2 C	Clearance obtained by Note (1) below	Clearance required in Yards	Compass Bearing				
1	R10a.96.55	2500	122	110	−12	431	2450	126	1700	111	107	80	43°	Table	5000	} Mathisen 121	No.1 Group (2/Lt L. Hall)
2	R10a.75.36	2350	122	114	−8	370	2350	126	1650	92	86	80	44°	fine	5250		
3	R10a.57.68	2400	117	123	+6	408	2400	129	1700	111	99	80	45°	fine	5000	} Mathisen 121	No.2 Group (2/Lt G.L. Rowe)
4	R10c.45.75	2400	116	126	+10	415	2450	134	1650	124	106	80	45°	shielded	5500		
5	R10c.70.00	2200	117	131	+14	311	2150	131	1450	68	54	40	40°30'	fine	5500	} Major O. 121	No.3 Group (Lt A.M.R. Bain. assisted by 2/Lt J.E. Ellis)
6	R9d.85.70	2100	116	133	+17	317	2200	133	1450	68	51	40	40°	per shielded	5000		
7	R9d.75.70	2150	116	136	+20	315	2200	135	1400	63	43	40	40°		4500		
8	R9d.70.75	2050	115	137	+22	309	2150	136	1400	63	41	40	39°30'	of Ellis	5750		

NOTES.—(1) CLEARANCE in yards = A − B plus or minus C according as trajectory tables give positive or negative values of C.
(2) IMMEDIATELY before firing Q.E. must be corrected, if necessary, for atmospheric influences. SEE TABLE 5.
(3) For lateral wind allowance. SEE TABLE 4.
(4) If obstruction exists between gun and target, and its highest point cannot be seen, ascertain if shots will clear by substituting "obstruction" for "own troops" in clearance columns above, and find clearance by rule in NOTE (1). Minimum clearance required equals half height of cone for range to obstruction.

INDIRECT OVERHEAD FIRE.

No. 1 2 0 M.G. Coy.　　No. 1.2.3.4. Section. S　　Date 5/6 May 1917.　　Map used 57 c. S.E. 10,000　　Officer i/c Firing LT. R.G. FRYER.

Gun No.	Target.	ELEVATION - Range to Target in Yards	Contours in Yards - Gun A	Contours in Yards - Target	V.I. in Yards	Q.E. in Minutes Table 3(A) or 3(B)	Range for Q.E. in Yards Table 1, Col. 2	CLEARANCE OVER OWN TROOPS - Contour of own troops in Yards B	Range to own troops in Yards	Traj. Height in Yards Table 2 C	Clearance obtained by Note (1) below	Clearance required in Yards	DIRECTION - Compass Bearing Reading	Time of firing	No. of rounds fired	Checked by	REMARKS. General.
9	R.8.4.70.15	2100	115	110	5	278	2050	132	1000	60	43	20	16°	as per attached table	5500		
10	R.8.6.80.15	2100	115	110	5	278	2050	132	1000	60	48	20	16°		5500		No. 4 Group. 2/Lt. Page.
11	R.8.6.90.35	1950	115	110	5	233	1900	132	1000	48	32	20	18°		5500		
12	R.8.6.85.35	1950	115	110	5	233	1900	132	1000	48	32	20	20°		5500		
13	R.9.6.80.50	2200	115	137	22	257	2300	132	1200	96	79	40	57°		3500		
14	R.9.c.70.50	2200	115	137	22	257	2300	132	1200	96	79	40	56°		4000		No. 5 Group. 2/Lt. R. Scott
15	R.9.c.55.60	2100	115	137	22	325	2200	132	1200	82.7	65.7	40	55°	do	5000		
16	R.9.c.40.60	2100	115	137	22	325	2200	132	1200	82.7	65.7	40	55°		4000		
17																	

NOTES.—(1) CLEARANCE in yards = A − B plus or minus C according as trajectory tables give positive or negative values of C.
(2) IMMEDIATELY before firing Q.E. must be corrected, if necessary, for atmospheric influences. SEE TABLE 5.
(3) For lateral wind allowance. SEE TABLE 4.
(4) If obstruction exists between gun and target, and its highest point cannot be seen, ascertain if shots will clear by substituting "obstruction" for "own troops" in clearance columns above, and find clearance by rule in NOTE (1). Minimum clearance required equals half height of cone for range to obstruction.

INDIRECT OVERHEAD FIRE.

No. 120 M.G. Coy. No. 1,2,3,4 Sections Date 5/6 May 1917 Map used 57.c.S.E.10,000 Officer i/c Firing Lt. R.G. FRYER

Gun No.	Target	ELEVATION — Range to Target in Yards	Contours in Yards — Gun A	Contours in Yards — Target	V.I. in Yards	Q.E. in Minutes Table 3(A) or 3(B)	Range for Q.E. in Yards Table 1, Col. 2	CLEARANCE OVER OWN TROOPS — Contour of own troops in Yards B	Range to own troops in Yards	Traj. Height in Yards Table 2 C	Clearance obtained by Note (1) below	Clearance required in Yards	DIRECTION — Compass Bearing True	Time of firing	No. of rounds fired	Checked by	REMARKS — General
17	Rg.c 55.25	1900	126½	137½	11	246	1950	137½	1000	52	41	20	90°		3250		
18	do	2000	126½	137½	11	274	2050	137½	1000	48.3	38.3	20	89°	As per attached time table	3250	Reg. ↑ Matheson 1/1	No. 6 Group 2/Lt Bennett
19	do	2100	126½	137½	11	305	2150	137½	1000	48.3	38.3	20	87°		3250		
20	Rg.d 5035	2200	126½	137½	11	339	2250	137½	1000	48.3	38.3	20	86°		3250		
21	R8.d 6050	1450	132	126	6	115	1400	115.5	700	33.3	49.8	20	89°		3250		
22	do	1550	132	126	6	133	1500	115.5	700	43.6	60.1	20	92°		3250	Maj. ? 2/c	No. 7 Group 2/Lt. Macfarlane
23	do	1650	132	132	0	155	1650	115.5	700	65.8	62.3	20	88°	as per sp	3250		
24	Rg.c 5050	1750	132	132	0	182	1750	115.5	700	79.1	95.6	20	87°		3250		

NOTES.—(1) CLEARANCE in yards = A − B plus or minus C according as trajectory tables give positive or negative values of C.
(2) IMMEDIATELY before firing Q.E. must be corrected, if necessary, for atmospheric influences. SEE TABLE 5.
(3) For lateral wind allowance. SEE TABLE 4.
(4) If obstruction exists between gun and target, and its highest point cannot be seen, ascertain if shots will clear by substituting "obstruction" for "own troops" in clearance columns above, and find clearance by rule in NOTE (1). Minimum clearance required equals half height of cone for range to obstruction.

SECRET.

Copy No. 5.

121st. INFANTRY BRIGADE ORDER No 93.

REFERENCE 57c. S.E. 1/10,000
and SPECIAL MAP (Issued only to
those concerned.)

5th May 1917.

1/ To impede the progress which the enemy is making in strengthening his position the 40th. Division will raid the LA VACQUERIE position, in conjunction with the 8th Division, on the 5th May (Z day). Zero hour will be 11.0. p.m.

2/ (a) The Raid will be carried out by the 119th Infantry Brigade on the Right and the 121st Infantry Brigade on the Left.

(b) The 120th Machine Gun Coy. is placed at the disposal of G.O.C. 121st Infantry Brigade.

(c) One Section, 4th Guards Machine Gun Coy. will remain in Second System.

3/ Boundaries.

The dividing line between 119th and 121st. Infantry Brigades will be from R.20.a.8.7. - R.15.c.0.4. - R.15.d.7.3. - the road thence past the Church to R.16.c.1.4. - R.16.c.7.3. all inclusive to the 121st Infantry Brigade.

4/ Covering Troops will be pushed forward to line as under (chain dotted line on map):-

119th. Infantry Brigade

R.22.b.00.55 along trench to R.22.a.5.6. to R.16.c.5.3.

121st Infantry Brigade.

R.16.c.5.3. - R.16.a.5.8. - R.16.a.1.1. - R.15.b.0.7. to present line.

5/ The Raid of the 121st Infantry Brigade will be carried out by the 20th Bn. Middlesex Regt. on the Right and 12th. Bn. Suffolk Regt. on the left.

6/ Junction of Battalions is shown on map.

The 20th. Bn. Middlesex Regt. being responsible for that

1.

portion of LA VACQUERIE allotted to the Brigade and the 12th. Bn. Suffolk Regt. for the enemy trench system in R.15. as shown on Special Map.

7. 20th. Bn. Middlesex Regt. will form up on the Left of 119th. Infantry Brigade and will conform to their advance.

12th. Bn. Suffolk Regt. will arrange positions of assembly in front of present line.

Both Battalions conforming closely to the creeping barrage.

8. Strong Mopping Up Parties will be detailed to follow each assaulting party.

Particular attention will be paid by O.C. 20th. Bn. Middlesex Regt. to Sunken Road, where covering post will be established about R.16.a.1.1., and by O.C. 12th. Bn. Suffolk Regt. to the Sunken Road through R.15.c. and d., and its defences which must be cleared without delay. Battalions will gain touch with one another about the point marked X on map.

9. The Infantry will be responsible for destroying, with 'P' Bombs, any dug-outs found and the R.E. for destroying all cellars, emplacements, etc.

10. O.C. 231st. Field Coy. R.E. will detail the necessary party to follow the mopping up party of 20th. Bn. Middlesex Regt. The Officer in charge of this party will report to O.C. 20th. Bn. Middlesex Regt. for instructions on receipt of these orders.

11. At 1 a.m. the 6th May the withdrawal of the 20th. Bn. Middlesex Regt. will commence in conjunction with 119th. Infantry Brigade. The O.C. Covering Troops will ensure that LA VACQUERIE is clear of all troops (including dead and wounded) before he withdraws. As soon as O.C. 12th Bn. Suffolk Regiment is satisfied that the 20th. Bn. Middlesex Regiment are clear of LA VACQUERIE, the withdrawal of the 12th. Bn. Suffolk Regt. will be commenced. The O.C. Covering Troops taking all measures to ensure the trenches are

clear of all men before withdrawal.

Brigade Head Quarters will be kept informed of progress and the completion of the withdrawal.

12. 21st Bn. Middlesex Regt. will move to old main line of Resistance and adjacent posts between about Q.35.a.0.0. and Q.29.c.0.3. by 10.0 p.m. Z day.

C.O. to report at Advanced Head Quarters at 10-45 P.M.

13. O.C. 121st Machine Gun Coy. will place 1 Section at the disposal of O.C. 12th Bn. Suffolk Regt. O.C. Section to report for instructions on receipt of these orders.

O.C. 121st Machine Gun Coy will arrange a machine gun barrage to cover the Left Flank of the advance with 2 Sections 121st Machine Gun Coy. and the 120th Machine Gun Coy. He will issue the necessary instructions direct to O.C. 120th Machine Gun Coy.

Details of Machine Gun Barrage will be issued to all concerned.

14. O.C. 121st Trench Mortar Batty. will place 2 guns at disposal of O.C. 12th. Bn. Suffolk Regt. to whom he will report for instructions on receipt of these orders.

15. Details regarding the Barrage and the action of the Artillery have been issued to all concerned.

16. <u>Distinguishing Marks.</u>

R.E. and Moppers Up will wear White armbands.

Men carrying wire cutters or breakers will wear a piece of white tape tied to the right shoulder strap.

Application will be made to Brigade Head Quarters for numbers of above required.

17. Os. C. 12th Bn. Suffolk Regt. and 20th Middlesex Regt. will send Liaison Officers to battalions on both flanks.

18. C.O's will ensure that Officers and men who take any part in the Raid leave all maps, orders and other documents behind them before the raid takes place.

19. O.C. 12th. Bn. Suffolk Regt. will ensure that the present Line of Resistance is adequately manned throughout the raid.

20. Any prisoners will be sent to Advanced Brigade Head Quarters.

21. Brigade Signal Officer will arrange to synchronise watches at Advanced Brigade Head Quarters at 3.0 p.m. and 6.0 p.m. on Z day.

22. Advanced Brigade Head Quarters will open at Q.29.a.9.5. (Sunken Road) at 6.0 p.m. on Z day.

23. Acknowledge.

D. J. Collins
Major,
Brigade Major,
121st. Infantry Brigade.

Issued at 8-30. a.m.

Copy No. 1 to O.C. 12th Bn. Suff R.
2. 13th Bn. York R.
3. 20th Bn. Midd R.
4. 21st Bn. Midd R.
5. 121st M.G. Coy.
6. 121st T. M. Batty
7. H.Q. 119th Inf. Bde.
8. 120th Inf Bde
9. 40th Divn (G)
10. O.C. Right Group R.A.
11. to O.C. Left Group, R.A.
12. C.R.A. 40th. Divn.
13. C.R.E. 40th. Divn.
14. O.C. 231st. Fd. Coy. R.E.
15. 120th M.G. Coy.
16. Brigade Signals
17. War Diary
18. War Diary
19. File.

MACHINE GUN BARRAGE.

1. Machine Guns will be divided into groups as shewn on sketch map.

2. They will fire on their barrage lines at the rate and time given in table below.

3.

Groups.	Rate of fire per minute.	Duration of fire.
1.2.3.	100	11.6 to 11.16
do	100	11.20 to 11.30
do	100	11.35 to 11.43
do	100	12 m.n. to 12.5
do	100	12.15 to 12.20
do	100	12.30 to 12.35
do	100	12.45 to 12.50
do	100	1.0 to 1.10
do	100	1.30 to 1.35
do	100	1.40 to 1.45
do	100	1.55 to 2.0
4.5.6.7.	50	11.0 to 11.43
do	50	11.50 to 12.30
do	75	12.30 to 1.0
do	50	1.5 to 1.30
1.2.3.4.5.6.7.	125	1.50 to 1.51
do	125	2.20 to 2.21
do	125	2.45 to 2.46
do	125	3.15 to 3.16

4. 8,500 rounds per gun, including S.A.A. in belts, will be at or close to the gun groups.

5. Condensers will be used and one petrol tin of water per pair of guns will be at the gun positions.

6. Guns will not traverse or search.

7. Illuminated aiming marks will be screened from enemy view.

(sgd) D.J. Collins

Major,
Brigade Major,
121st. Infantry Brigade.

5th May, 1917.

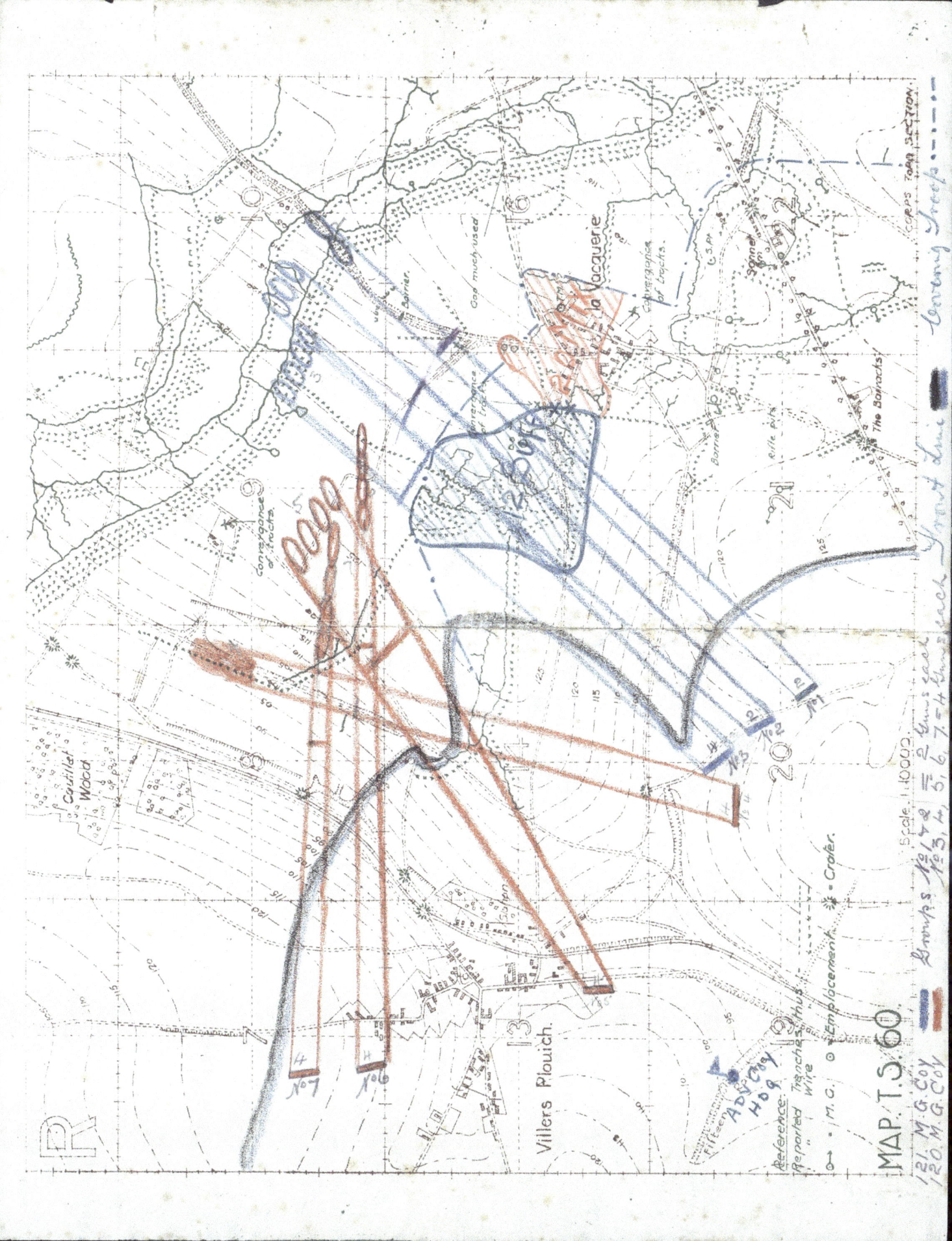

Vol 13

CONFIDENTIAL. 121 Machine Gun Company.

WAR DIARY.

VOLUME 12.

June 1917

Army Form C. 2118.

Page 1

WAR DIARY
or
INTELLIGENCE SUMMARY.
(Erase heading not required.)

Place	Date	Hour	Summary of Events and Information	Remarks and references to Appendices
DESSART WOOD	June 1st		Friday. Enemy very quiet all day. 5 guns fires indirect fire from R.6.a. on to targets about R.15. Central (LA VACQUERIE). 15000 rounds fire. No observation of results obtained. Lt ROWE proceeded to "B" Battery R.F.A. 181 Bde for a two days course on General Artillery work. 2/Lt V.R. HEMBROW proceeded to the Machine Gun Base on being appointed Permanent Base Officer and was struck off strength of the Company. Strength of the Company 9 Officers 161 O.R. Weather very fine.	Map GONNELIEU 57cSE/1 10000
	June 2		Saturday. Enemy quiet as usual. Orders were issued that this Company is to be relieved by the 119th M.G. Company tonight. This was carried out Headquarters and transport did not move, the teams came back to bivouacs in the wood. One man from each team remained with teams of 119 by and regimen up in the morning. N° 9 Section occupies Weather raining.	

A5834 Wt.W4973/M687 750,000 8/16 D.D.&L.Ltd. Forms/C.2118/13.

Army Form C. 2118.

Page 2

WAR DIARY
or
INTELLIGENCE SUMMARY.
(Erase heading not required.)

Place	Date	Hour	Summary of Events and Information	Remarks and references to Appendices
DESSART WOOD	June 2		Saturday (cont) occupied 4 positions in the BROWN LINE (Corps defence line).	
	June 3		Sunday 3/15 male proceed to C Battery 181 Bde R.F.A.. The Company cleaned up all day. The afternoon and evening was Enemy aeroplanes very Company was busy in the evening. We had 2 gas alarm and has to active at 11 p.m. This moved to a false alarm. Turn all the men. We were ordered to stand to on the S.O.S. at 2/15 am we went up from the right Battalion left Bde front Signal Machines developed.	
	June 4		Monday Started a programme of work which includes from 5-6 hours work this day. 2/15 A.P. male was wounded this afternoon in the left shoulder near FIFTEEN RAVINE and was admitted to hospital. No 2 Sec in reliver No 1 Section in the BROWN LINE. Weather fine.	

Army Form C. 2118.

Coys. 3

WAR DIARY
or
INTELLIGENCE SUMMARY.
(Erase heading not required.)

Instructions regarding War Diaries and Intelligence Summaries are contained in F. S. Regs., Part II. and the Staff Manual respectively. Title pages will be prepared in manuscript.

Place	Date	Hour	Summary of Events and Information	Remarks and references to Appendices
DESSART WOOD	June 5th		Tuesday. Continued with programme of work. Nos 3 & 4 Sections were on the range all morning. Weather fine.	
	June 6th		Wednesday. Training continued. No 3 Section relieved No 2 Section in the BROWN LINE. Weather fine.	
	June 7th		Thursday. The Company had baths at FINS this morning. No 4 Section has to return No 3 Section for a short time to enable them to get a bath. The Court Martial on Sgt Ward was held at the H.Q. 20th Bn Middlesex Regt this morning. Weather fine.	
	June 8th		Friday. C.O. and Sgt McCarthy left the Company this morning for a machine gun course at CAMIERS. Lt D.J. AMERY-PARKES which over command of the Company and Lt A.M.R. BAIN took over the duties of Second-in-Command.	

WAR DIARY or INTELLIGENCE SUMMARY

Place	Date	Hour	Summary of Events and Information	Remarks and references to Appendices
DESSART WOOD	June 8th		Friday (continued) No. 4 Section relieves No. 3 Section in the BROWN LINE. 3 O.R. joins the Company from the Base.	
	June 9th		Saturday. Training continued. O.C. & 2/c went up to reconnoitre the GONNELIEU SECTOR and make arrangements for the relief of 180 M.G. Coy. The following night to be sent up — L/Sgt Leake L/Sgt " Grun Cpl " Type Frean L/Cpl " L/Cpl Foote L/Cpl No front line gun positions have been made.	
	June 10th		Sunday. The usual divine service in the morning. The Company relieves the 180 M.G. Coy in the GONNELIEU SECTOR. Relief started at 10 pm, 8 guns in the line, and was over by 1 am. 4 guns in the Front line 4 guns in the Intermediate line	

Army Form C. 2118.

Page 5.

WAR DIARY
or
INTELLIGENCE SUMMARY

(Erase heading not required.)

Place	Date	Hour	Summary of Events and Information	Remarks and references to Appendices
GONNELIEU	June 10th		Sunday (continued) 3 Guns at H.Q. Headquarters. W.6.c.8.1. Transport bivouac. This sector is a very large one and the guns are a long distance apart. The defence of the immediate line is very good as well; the front line appears to have no defence at all; although the defence scheme states that the front line will be held at all costs. Enemy shells GONNELIEU occasionally.	Map 57 c S.E. 1/20000. Offensive & Disposition Map.
	June 11th		Monday Weather Fine.	
	June 12th		Tuesday Enemy quiet. 1 S.A. Wamn returns from leave. 2/Lt R.G. Reinman joins the Company for duty from the Base. Weather Fine.	
	June 13th		Wednesday Enemy quiet, except for a certain amount of aerial activity. 4 Guns carried out night firing from R.26.c.&.d on to trenches and road north about LA VACQUERIE, about	

Army Form C. 2118.

Page 46

WAR DIARY
or
INTELLIGENCE SUMMARY
(Erase heading not required.)

Place	Date	Hour	Summary of Events and Information	Remarks and references to Appendices
GONNELIEU (cont)	June 13		Wednesday. About 8000 rounds were fired. 13 O.R. joins the Company from the Base.	
	June 14th		Thursday. C.O. went round the Sector with the Bde. Major and arranged various alterations in the defence viz 2 more guns in the Front line to even the eff. of the S.M. Battalion and a reduction in the intermediate line from 9 guns to 6 guns. this gives 1 complete Section in reserve. Enemy quiet. Weather fine.	
	June 15th		Friday. Enemy fairly quiet. Shells GOUZEAUCOURT in the afternoon. Usual night firing was carried out. Work on the new emplacements in the Front line was started.	
	June 16th		Saturday. C.O. attended a conference at Reserve Bde H.Q. The night by Lg Gun of the Front line still fairly quiet. Gas from Trench Mortar Gas fired 9 men in morning.	

Army Form C. 2118.

WAR DIARY
or
INTELLIGENCE SUMMARY.
(Erase heading not required.)

Instructions regarding War Diaries and Intelligence Summaries are contained in F. S. Regs., Part II. and the Staff Manual respectively. Title pages will be prepared in manuscript.

Page 7

Place	Date	Hour	Summary of Events and Information	Remarks and references to Appendices
GONNELIEU	June 16th		Saturday (cont.) Usual night firing carries on.	
	June 17th		Sunday. Usual night firing carries on. Weather fine. Enemy shells GONNELIEU. 2 m.g. guns were placed in the Front line. Night firing carried out on the CAMBRAI road. 2/15 HULL proceeded on leave to U.K.	
	June 18th		Monday. Stormy weather. Enemy quiet. Stokes battery new by LA VACQUERIE. H.Q. further up the road. Night firing on LA VACQUERIE.	
	June 19th		Tuesday. Weather wet. Enemy quiet. Moved into new by H.Q. Usual night firing on LA VACQUERIE.	
	June 20th		Wednesday. Enemy shells QUARRY, GOUZEAUCOURT, weather wet. Enemy replaces on PAVÉ ROAD 2/15 Robinson 2 guns carried out by O.C. 11th K.O.R.L. Night firing as usual.	
	June 21st		Thursday. Weather wet. Usual night firing. 2/15 I.W. Bourke joined the company. Aircraft active during the evening from the	

M. G. Boy. Sgt.

A5834 Wt. W4973/M687 750,000 8/16 D. D. & L. Ltd. Forms/C.2118/13.

Army Form C. 2118.

Page 8

WAR DIARY
or
INTELLIGENCE SUMMARY.
(Erase heading not required.)

Instructions regarding War Diaries and Intelligence Summaries are contained in F.S. Regs., Part II. and the Staff Manual respectively. Title pages will be prepared in manuscript.

Place	Date	Hour	Summary of Events and Information	Remarks and references to Appendices
GONNELIEU	June 23rd		**Saturday** Weather fine but cold. Usual night firing on and nightfarees. Enemy very quiet.	
	June 24th		**Sunday** Weather fine. New front line in front of GONNELIEU was commenced about 150-200 yds in front of the present line. Major LACEY 120 M.G. Company was appointed Divisional Machine Gun Officer. This appointment will greatly facilitate the work on offensive lines on the line and will ensure the cooperation which is at present lacking. Enemy very quiet.	
			Monday Weather fine. All Machine Gun emplacements were manned with fine Lewis Boards containing Tactical Cards, Sketches of field of fire and Trench Store Cards.	
	June 26th		**Tuesday** Weather fine. The company was relieved by the 119th M.G. Company (S.B.) Relief started at 10 pm and was complete by 1am (S.B.) After relief the company moved to W.T.6.5.8. where it was accommodated in tents taken over from 119	

A5834 Wt. W4973/M687 750,000 8/16 D. D. & L. Ltd. Forms/C.2118/13.

Army Form C. 2118.

Page 9.

WAR DIARY
or
INTELLIGENCE SUMMARY.
(Erase heading not required.)

Place	Date	Hour	Summary of Events and Information	Remarks and references to Appendices
DESSART VALLEY	June 26th		Tuesday 119 M.G. Company.	
	27th		Wednesday Coy Company Res Cadres at FINS in the morning after which they cleaned up. 2/Lt S.A. Wann left this morning for ABBEVILLE to bring remounts for the Division from the Remount Office there. The Company was here up in the evening. Weather fine	
	28th		Thursday A Programme of work was chalked this morning. Today Programme comprised Gun Drill - Stoppages - Pack Animal Drill - Range Cards Jams & 1st Inspection at B30. H.Q. at 5 p.m. C.O. attended a Conference	
	29th		Friday Weather fine. C.O. went round the VILLERS GUISLAIN Sector with the Brigade Major and reconnoitred the M.G. positions.	
	30th		Saturday C.O. reconnoitred the GAUCHE WOOD Sector. Orders were received that this Coy was to relieve the 35th Division on the 1/2nd & 2/3rd July.	

A5834. Wt.W4923/M687 750,000 8/16 D.D.& L. Ltd. Forms/C.2118/13.

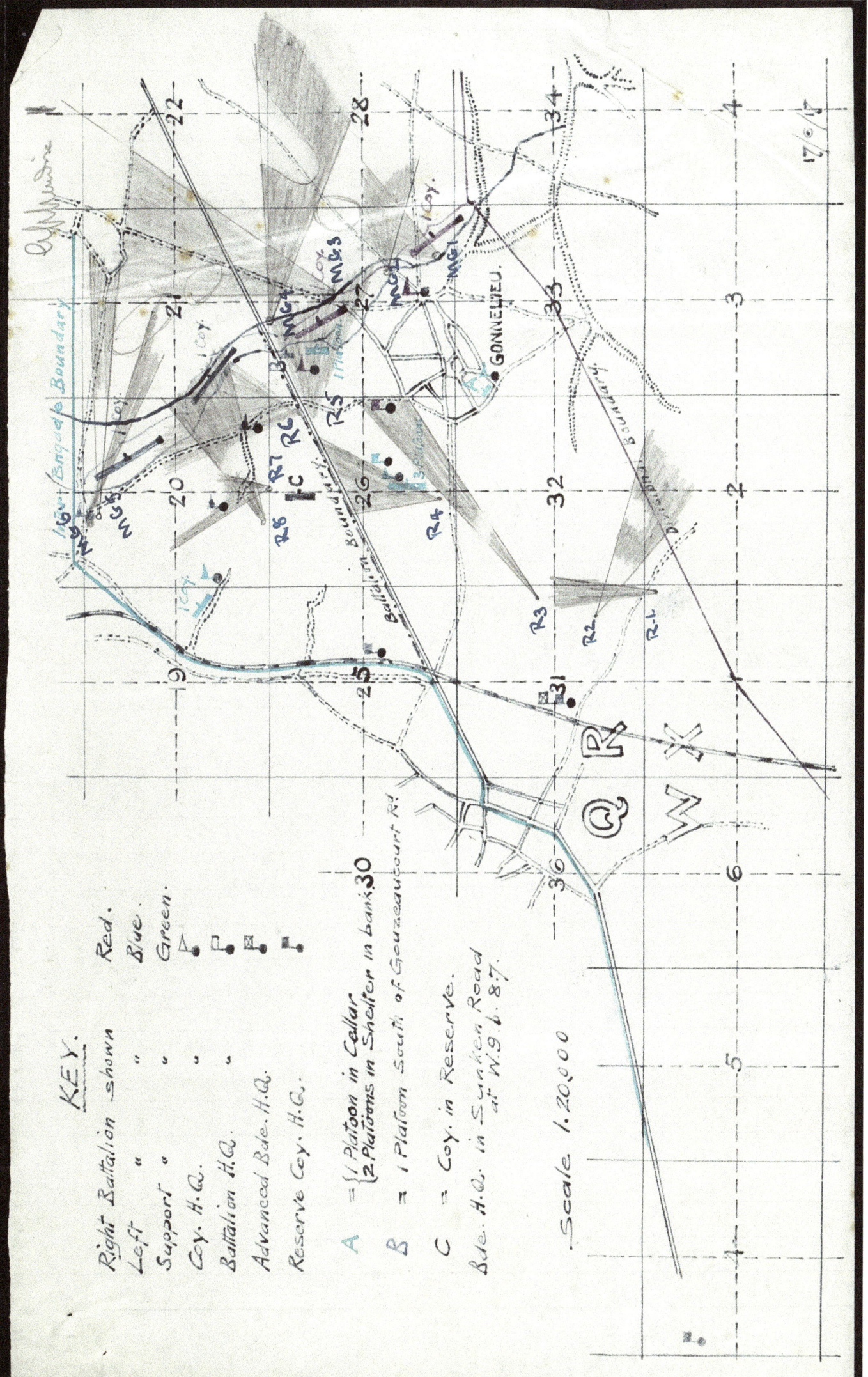

Army Form C. 2118.

WAR DIARY
or
INTELLIGENCE SUMMARY.
(Erase heading not required.)

Place	Date	Hour	Summary of Events and Information	Remarks and references to Appendices
			JUNE 1917.	
			Reinforcements	
			Nº 63450 Pte Penta. T. ⎱ June 6ᵗʰ 1917	
			29022 L/Cpl Savage R. ⎰	
			29139 Pte Yelles J.W. June 6ᵗʰ 1917	
			2/15 R.G. Robinson from Base Depot June 12ᵗʰ.	
			Nº 9051 L/Cpl Brown. W.	
			82115 Thomas. G.G.	
			81508 Young H.	
			67005 Cannon a.	
			14538 Samuels. J. ⎱ June 13 1917.	
			68470 Amos W.C.	
			57568 Powell E.	
			6471 Rush R.	
			90538 Gregory W.E.	

WAR DIARY
or
INTELLIGENCE SUMMARY.
(Erase heading not required.)

Army Form C. 2118.

Place	Date	Hour	Summary of Events and Information	Remarks and references to Appendices
			To Hospital	
			46552 Pte Burgess. A. 3-6-17. 29094 Pte Oyles. D. 16-6-17	
			25685 " Kirby. C. 4-6-17 29093 Sgt Keogh. P. 16-6-17	
			43410 " Darby. J. 16-6-17 6702 Pte Watson. J. 18-6-17	
			30070 " Fenton. W. 14-6-17 25704 Dr Jammy ⎫ 18-6-17	
			60575 " Bailey 23-6-17 Lt. C.L. Rivers ⎬ 22-6-17	
			29663 " Monks A. 14-6-17 Pte Dupres (Bat man) 3-6-17	
			59126 " Morris. J. 30-6-17 Pte Lawrence 63545 R 30-6-17	
			To Camiers	
			Major P. Matheson CAMIERS 8-6-17.	
			(Batman Pte Thurston)	
			Sgt McCarthy ABBEVILLE 8-6-17.	
			29011 Dr Gant CAMIERS 28-6-17.	
			32071 Sgt Lloyd 30-6-17	
			30743 Cpl Young " 30-6-17	
			45276	

WAR DIARY
or
INTELLIGENCE SUMMARY.
(Erase heading not required.)

Army Form C. 2118.

Place	Date	Hour	Summary of Events and Information	Remarks and references to Appendices
			From Hospital.	
			28999 L/Cpl Watin T. 1-6-17 3741 Cpl Green T. 9-6-17	
			18961 Dr Peterman S.W. 1-6-17 84463 Pte Andrews 10-6-17	
			11449 Dr Willis A. 1-6-17 85750 Johnston 13-6-17	
			29041 Pte Mahon P. 2-6-17 29563 Munro 26-6-17	
			29042 " Lambert J 6-6-17 60575 Bailey 27-6-17	
			25687 " Kirby 7-6-17 30070 Fenton 17-6-17	
			2/5 A.P. Male 43410 Davey 20-6-17	
			64603 Pte Wise 29-6-17.	
			Strength Decrease.	
			2/5 Y.P. Henderson to Base 1-6-17	
			2/5 A.P. Mole Wounded 3-6-17	
			87307 Pte Andrews to Reinforcements 11-6-17	
			C.Q.M.S. Hugell Sent to 130 M.G. Coy 24-6-17	
			46552 Pte. Burgess. Q. R Evacuated 10-6-17.	

WAR DIARY
or
INTELLIGENCE SUMMARY.
(Erase heading not required.)

Army Form C. 2118.

Reinforcements
Nº 90638   (enl) Gregory
   90630   Pte Milford W.E.
   91019   " Steed - Millbank W.
   92614   " Head. S.
   85259   " Withers. R. G.
            " McPhee. Q.
   20 -
   29701   Sgt Orr. H.   — June 18 1917
   18427   C.Q.M.S. Smith. J.   June 21st 1917
   10938   Cpl Kellender. J.   June 29

From leave
21690 Sgt Brennen   8-6-17
  "   S.A. Wann   13-6-17
29563 Pte Montes   15-6-17
26096 Pte Sweeney   18-6-17
 9565 Pte Cook   18-6-17
29047 Pte Bagley   21-6-17

                    25692 HQ Drake 21-6-17
                    2155 A.R. Mule 22-6-17
                    29031 Pte Goodfellow 22-6-17

From Courses
25696 Pte Davis 9-6-17

June 13 1917

Original Copy

Vol 14

Confidential

War Diary
of
121 Coy Machine Gun Corps

From 1st July 1917 To 31st July 1917

Volume 13

Army Form C. 2118.

WAR DIARY
or
INTELLIGENCE SUMMARY.
(Erase heading not required.)

Place	Date	Hour	Summary of Events and Information	Remarks and references to Appendices
VILLERS-GUISLAIN	1/7/17		The O.C. Coy returned from M.G. Course at CAMIERS. The Coy has relieved the 105 & 106 Bde's M.G. Corps in the VILLERS-GUISLAIN, GAUCHE WOOD sectors. Fourteen guns in the Line on a 4000 yds front, 2 in reserve. Relief complete 1 a.m. 2/7/17. From Leave:- 2/Lt. D.M. Hall & No. 14358 L/Cpl. McCarthy.E. From Course:- Major O. Mathieson, No.29011 Sgt. McCarthy.M, No.13302 Pte Thorsen, H.P. On Courses:- No. 30743. Sgt. J. Lloyds. Weather. Dull. Fair.	
	2/7/17		The guns have been disposed as follows:- Front Gun System. M.G's 2, 3, 5, 7. & L. 1, 2, 3, 4. Support Gun System. M.G's 8 & 9. Reserve Line (Reserve) M.G's 3, 4, 6 & 8. Coy Head qrs are at X.9.d. 50,50. Transport & D.H. Stores SOREL. Enemy very quiet On covers:- No. 45283. L/Cpl. Thristan O. Weather wet.	
	3/7/17		Enemy have been very quiet. Night firing was carried	

Army Form C. 2118.

WAR DIARY
or
INTELLIGENCE SUMMARY.
(Erase heading not required.)

Instructions regarding War Diaries and Intelligence Summaries are contained in F.S. Regs., Part II. and the Staff Manual respectively. Title pages will be prepared in manuscript.

Place	Date	Hour	Summary of Events and Information	Remarks and references to Appendices
VILLERS-GUISLAIN	3/7/17		on HONNECOURT with 4 guns. Result good. Enemy retaliated with about 300 shells but did no damage. Leave. N° 33305. Bdr. J. Roxborough. N° 37756. Gnr. Thirsk. Weather fine.	
	4/7/17		Enemy have been very active at TURNERS QUARRY. 4 Guns carried out night firing on various targets. Reinforcements:- N° 10214. Gnr. J. Willard. N° 25902 Gnr. R. Gogg. N° 13706. Dr. J. Johnson. Lt. G. L. Carr returned from Hospital. N° 29700. Gnr. H. Dupency. Returned from leave. Dr. N° 4035832 Wilson. J. Gnr. Barnes. N° 33250. Gnr. Steel. B.	
	5/7/17		Enemy have been shelling TURNERS QUARRY + left of sector. The Div. M.G. Officer has been round the sector with the O.C. Bty. Night firing has been carried out with 4 guns on HONNECOURT. Weather fine.	
	6/7/17		The enemy has been rather quieter today. Nightfiring with 4 guns was carried out on CANAL BRIDGES FRANQUEVILLE. Leave. N° 29034. Gnr. G. Bryson. Weather fine.	

Army Form C. 2118.

WAR DIARY
or
INTELLIGENCE SUMMARY.
(Erase heading not required.)

Place	Date	Hour	Summary of Events and Information	Remarks and references to Appendices
VILLERS-GUISLAIN.	7/7/17		The enemy have been very quiet. 4 guns nights firing on THICKET FARM. Lt. G. L. Rhue wounded. Leave:- N° 29038. Gnr. Burrow. J. On leave:- N° 27695. Pte. G. Tucker. Trombours. N° 45283. L/Cpl. O. Thruston. Weather Wet.	
	8/7/17		Enemy very quiet. The usual night firing has been carried out on LES TRANCHEES & HONNECOURT with success. The enemy retaliated with about 400 shells of various calibre up to 5.9 also with gas shells. Weather fine.	
	9/7/17		Enemy has been very quiet. No night firing owing to Infantry relief. Weather very fine. 2 Lt. J. Thorpe admitted to Hospital sick. On leave. N° 29081. Pte. W. Barni.	
	10/7/17		Enemy very quiet. No night firing. Gunny Brust now a rest. C.O.R's sent to Base as inefficient. On leave.— N° 18427. Q.M. Sgt. Smith. N° 24497. Pte. G. Goodall. Weather fine. O.C. proceeded on leave	
	11/7/17		The enemy has been very quiet.	

Army Form C. 2118.

WAR DIARY
or
INTELLIGENCE SUMMARY.
(Erase heading not required.)

Place	Date	Hour	Summary of Events and Information	Remarks and references to Appendices
VILLERS - GUISLAIN.	11/7/17		To the O.K. Night firing was carried out on FRANQUEVILLE with 4 Guns. Weather fine.	
	12/7/17		The enemy artillery has been very active on Right Bat. front. Registration apparently being carried out. At about 12.5 a.m. (13th) a heavy bombardment was opened on the Right Bat. front. Our mg's firing guns, firing on THICKET FARM withdrew to their Battle Emplacements in the GREEN LINE, nothing further transpired. Guns Lewis. No. 36029. L.S.M. Knok & No. 29028 Sgt. Montgomery. Weather fine.	
	13/7/17		The enemy have been very quiet. The 60th M.G. Officers paid a short visit. The usual night firing with 4 guns was carried out on HONNECOURT & Canal Bridges. Weather fine.	
	14/7/17		The sector has been very, very quiet. Night firing was carried out on 2 Enemy Posts off FIFE RD. in conjunction	

Army Form C. 2118.

WAR DIARY
or
INTELLIGENCE SUMMARY.
(Erase heading not required.)

Instructions regarding War Diaries and Intelligence Summaries are contained in F. S. Regs., Part II. and the Staff Manual respectively. Title pages will be prepared in manuscript.

Place	Date	Hour	Summary of Events and Information	Remarks and references to Appendices
VILLERS - GUISLAIN.	14/7/17		with 20th Middlesex Regt. Enemy retaliated. Weather fine.	
	15/7/17		The enemy very quiet. Usual M.Guns & Rifle fring on BOSQUET FARM. Leave:- N°. 14576. Pte. W. Holland. Weather fine.	
	16/7/17		The enemy quiet. Night firing was carried out on enemy trenches at R.29. c. & D. Returned from Leave. 2.O.R's. Work on Emplacement has progressed rapidly. Weather Wet.	
	17/7/17		The enemy Artillery has been more active. Night firing in conjunction with "B" Battery 296 Att. Bde. was carried out on HONNECOURT WOOD & Ahu switched on to Canal Bridge. Reinforcements from Base. 2/Lt G. P. Chapman. Weather Wet.	
	18/7/17		The weather has been very wet. Enemy very quiet. Night firing was carried out on Enemy trenches at R.29.c & D. Wet & Dull weather prevent us using a day sniping gun.	

Army Form C. 2118.

WAR DIARY
or
INTELLIGENCE SUMMARY.
(Erase heading not required.)

Instructions regarding War Diaries and Intelligence Summaries are contained in F. S. Regs., Part II. and the Staff Manual respectively. Title pages will be prepared in manuscript.

Place	Date	Hour	Summary of Events and Information	Remarks and references to Appendices
VILLERS-GUISLAIN	19/7/17		The enemy have been very quiet. Night firing was carried out on enemy Heavy. T.M. in R.28.D. with complete success, causing it to cease fire. Day firing has been carried out on enemy trenches R.39. c & D & Roads. Returned from leave. 3 O.R's. Weather Wet.	
	20/7/17		The enemy are very quiet. The Left Battn are now withdrawing Infantry from front line in day time & M.G.'s open fire to cover withdrawal at Stand Down & also to open fire & cover advance into front line at "Stand To". Night firing has been carried out on BUSQUET FARM. Weather Wet.	
	21/7/17		Enemy very quiet. Night firing on Heavy. T.M's in R.28.c. with 4 guns. From leave 1 O.R. On bonus E.S.M. Look. H. Enemy Artillery more active. Registration by day has been carried out by 2 guns. Night firing on LES TRANCHEES	
	22/7/17			

WAR DIARY or INTELLIGENCE SUMMARY

Army Form C. 2118.

Place	Date	Hour	Summary of Events and Information	Remarks and references to Appendices
VILLERS-GUISLAIN	22/7/17			
	23/7/17		Weather fine. Enemy Artillery has been active. 2 Guns fired by day on enemy Heavy T.M's which fire on FAWCUS AVEN, from H.00 onwards. Night firing was carried on on Heavy T.M's in R.28.d. Returned from Leave. Q.M.S. Smith J.R. Weatherhie.	
	24/7/17		The O.C. Coy returned from leave. Night & Day firing has been carried out & Honnecourt Wood has been thoroughly searched. Enemy Artillery has been less active. Weather fine.	
	25/7/17		The Enemy Artillery has been very active with 5.9, 77 m.m., Gas shells & Heavy T.M's on TURNERS QUARRY & Left section also was in front of Right Batt'y. They also carried our counter battery work. About 5/6 n. m enemy Deserter came over & reported that a raid would take place at 3/4 a.m. 28th on Right Batt'y front.	

Army Form C. 2118.

WAR DIARY
or
INTELLIGENCE SUMMARY.
(Erase heading not required.)

Instructions regarding War Diaries and Intelligence Summaries are contained in F. S. Regs., Part II. and the Staff Manual respectively. Title pages will be prepared in manuscript.

Place	Date	Hour	Summary of Events and Information	Remarks and references to Appendices
VILLERS-GUISLAIN	25/7/17		Lt. I.D. Strong Parker has been transferred to 119 Bty. M.G. Corps to take command from this date. Weather fine.	
	26/7/17		At 6 a.m. the enemy raid my trenches on Right front. Assisted by no less than six tombardiers having got in & captured about 21 O.R's & inflicted about 36 casualties. Approximately six opponents I attached. Lt E. C. Herbert reported for duty as 2nd i/c to replace Lt. 119 I.D. Strong Parker transferred to 119 M.G. Bty. The enemy have been very quiet all day. Enemy aircraft have been very active. Weather fine. Reinforcements 4 O.R's	No. 1 Ref. Enemy Raid
	27/7/17		Enemy very quiet. Night firing has been stopped for 2 nights. Work on emplacements is progressing rapidly. Weather fine. From Bourne S.S.M. I. Luck On leave. 3741 L/Sgt Green to M.G. School Camiers.	
	28/7/17		Enemy very quiet. 1 Bde on our right (35 Div) carried out a successful raid on enemy trenches about 2.30 a.m. Night firing was carried on in conjunction with a small raid by 21 on Middlesex on an enemy post. Return fire Feeble.	

Army Form C. 2118.

WAR DIARY
or
INTELLIGENCE SUMMARY.
(Erase heading not required.)

Place	Date	Hour	Summary of Events and Information	Remarks and references to Appendices
VILLERS - GUISLAIN	28/7/17		No 14376 Pte. Holland. W. Weather fine.	
	29/7/17		Enemy very quiet. Work is progressing very rapidly. Stores drawn No 30743 Sgt. J. Lloyd No 45-276-614. Young J. Our Artillery fired a 1 minute concentration on BLEAK TRENCH at 9.30 p.m. The 104 Bde, 35 Div carried out a raid on the enemy trenches. Weather wet.	
	30/7/17		Enemy very quiet. Work on emplacements etc is being carried on. Weather dull. Night firing was carried out.	
	31/7/17		Enemy very quiet. 2 Officers & 2 N.C.O's have been attached for duty from the Div (244) M.G. Coy for instruction. The usual night firing has been carried out. Weather fine.	

In the Field
31/7/17

Mathisen Major
Commanding 121 Coy M.G. Corps

Appendix I

Copy of Daily Report   25/7/17./26/7/17.

No night firing was done by this Company last night. At about 6.a.m. this morning enemy opened fire on Villers Guislain - batteries in rear with 5.9" shells. Two minutes later the Right Battalion Front came under heavy bombardment, principally on the Right Company's Sector, heavy T.M's were the principle missiles.

The Section Officers at once proceeded to Battle Stations and the following Guns fired;

M.G. 2.	1,000 rounds	on	Alternative Line
3A	3,000 "	"	S.O.S. "
3.	4,000 "	"	S.O.S. "
5.	3,000 "	"	Alternative "
7.	4,500 "	"	S.O.S. "
8.	4,500 "	"	Alternative "

No communication was established with Company concerned and Section Officers and N.C.O's. used their own initiative; communication was however kept with Right Battalion Hqrs. Owing to mist and smoke from barrage no observation could be obtained. The Guns fired until situation became more quiet.

M.G.2. Gun fired very badly and broke all spare firing pins - the Gun was out of action for about 20 minutes until a firing pin could be obtained from another Gun. A new Gun from Vaucellette Farm is replacing this Gun tonight. M.G.3. position was persistently shelled throughout and is obviously known to the enemy; I beg to recommend that this Gun be moved tonight to vicinity of M.G.4. position near Artillery O.P.

I am of opinion that no other Guns were spotted and owing to the intensity of the bombardment the Machine Guns could hardly be heard firing at all.

Casualties   nil.

26-7-17.

P. Mathison
signed   Major.
Commanding 121st Company Machine Gun Corps

WAR DIARY
or
INTELLIGENCE SUMMARY.
(Erase heading not required.)

Army Form C. 2118.

Place	Date	Hour	Summary of Events and Information	Remarks and references to Appendices

For Month ending 31st July 1917

Casualties:-

	Officers	N.C.O.S	O.Rs.
Killed	—	—	1
Wounded	1	1	2
Hospital	2	1	10

Total 15

Reinforcements

Officers	2
N.C.O.S	1
O.Rs.	7

Total. 9

Indirect Fire.

Number of Guns engaged.   Totals 102
Expenditure of S.A.A.   290,750 rds
Number of Targets Engaged.   99.
Average per Gun per night.   about 2,850 rds.

In the Field
31st July 1917

G. Mathieson Major
O.C. 121 Coy M.G. Corps

Original copy

Vol 15

Confidential.

War Diary
- of -
121st. Company Machine Gun Corps

From 1st August 1917 To 31st August 1917.

Volumen 14

Army Form C. 2118.

WAR DIARY
or
INTELLIGENCE SUMMARY.
(Erase heading not required.)

Instructions regarding War Diaries and Intelligence Summaries are contained in F. S. Regs., Part II. and the Staff Manual respectively. Title pages will be prepared in manuscript.

Place	Date	Hour	Summary of Events and Information	Remarks and references to Appendices
GONNELIEU & VILLE GUISLAIN	1.8.17		The enemy has been very quiet. 104 M.G. Coy relieved the guns at M.G. 2 M.G. 3 M.G. 4 & 41. 104 Bde has taken over the night sector of 121 Bde & 121 Bde is taking over the night sector of 119 Bde. Night firing was carried out. 2 Officers & 2 N.C.O.s attached for instruction from No 244 M.G. Coy. Weather wet. 2nd LIEUT J.W. BANKS admitted to hospital sick. Pte J.C. BUTLER 62965 accompanied 2nd/LIEUT BANKS as batman. No 28206 Pte COOKE. R. reinforcement from No 2 A.S.C. Section A.H.T.D	
	2.8.17		Coy. H.Q. moved to GUN LANE at x 7 b. 4 guns relieved 4 guns 119th M.G. Coy in the front line GONNELIEU & guns of 244 Coy relieved 4 guns of 119 M.G. Coy in the reserve line GONNELIEU. Enemy very quiet. Weather wet. 4 men of Pte W.H. JOHNSON No 88750	
	3.8.17		Enemy very quiet. Men in usual condition. Work on guns and ammunition, shelters &c rapidly progressing. Weather wet.	
	4.8.17		O.C. Coy went round the line with the G.O.C. & arrangements made to improve the dispositions of guns. Night firing was carried out. Internal Coy Relief. Weather wet. To hospital sick No 29012 Pte QUALEY.I & No 67005 Pte CAMERON.A.	

Army Form C. 2118.

WAR DIARY
or
INTELLIGENCE SUMMARY.
(Erase heading not required.)

Instructions regarding War Diaries and Intelligence Summaries are contained in F.S. Regs., Part II. and the Staff Manual respectively. Title pages will be prepared in manuscript.

Place	Date	Hour	Summary of Events and Information	Remarks and references to Appendices
GONNELIEU & VILLERS GUISLAIN	5.8.17		The S.O.S. lines & all guns attend & much laid out. Night firing carried out by N.O. moved to QUENTIN MILL. Weather wet. Reinforcements:- N° 29086 Pte POWELL. A. from Base. To hospital:- N° 27699 Corpl DALY. J. Strength decrease N° 29087 Pte ADAMS. J. to A.O.C. CALDELIEURE CALAIS courses N° 54823 Pte ARMIGER. C.V. to PERONNE Sanitary School Courses	
	6.8.17		A new emplacement for M.G. 3 under construction. Night firing carried out. Guns cleaned & inspected & new sight lines laid out. Weather:- fair. Lieut A.H. ALLIERS joined the Coy from Base. To hospital:- N° 82365 Pte LOWRY. G. Leave to U.K. N° 70376 Pte WOODWARD. W.	
	7.8.17		Enemy very quiet. Night firing & fresh stations as the carried out every attack night. Work on new emplacements carried out. Weather miserable, rain during greater part of the day. To hospital N° 55897 Pte LAWSON. H.	
	8.8.17		Enemy very quiet. New emplacement completed & occupied. Attacks on movements on our construction for M.G. 2 & M.G. 3 further firing carried out. Weather changeable. Rain during & clear from hospital N° 44318 Pte FISHKIN. R. To hospital N° 97674 Pte WITHERS. R. To U.K. N° 33227 Pte PARMENTER B.E. On leave to U.K. N° 30065 Pte COLE. H.	

Army Form C. 2118.

WAR DIARY
or
INTELLIGENCE SUMMARY.
(Erase heading not required.)

Instructions regarding War Diaries and Intelligence Summaries are contained in F. S. Regs., Part II. and the Staff Manual respectively. Title pages will be prepared in manuscript.

Place	Date	Hour	Summary of Events and Information	Remarks and references to Appendices
GONNELIEU & VILLERS GUISLAIN	8.8.16		Maj. M⁶⁴ withdrawn from the front line to relieve 2nd M.S. Coy in positions R14, R24 M.64 R2 & R3 position occupied by Lewis guns.	
	9.8.16		Enemy quiet. Men moved. Work on emplacements rapidly proceeding. 52 men to be permanently attached for transport duties at Transport Lines by order of the Div. General. 15 men to be attached to the Coy from Battalions. Weather changeable. From hospital :- No 97674 Pte WITHERS R. - No 52365 Pte LOWERY G.	
	10.8.16		Enemy very quiet. Work progressing rapidly. Night firing carried out. Weather fine. To hospital :- No 14238 Cpl McCARTHY E.	
	11.8.17		Enemy very quiet. 15 O.R. from Battalions reported for duty. Work progressing. Weather wet. No 54823 Pte ARMIGER C.V. returned from SANITARY SCHOOL PERONNE.	
	12.8.17		O.C. Coy inspected transport & men attached men. Enemy very quiet. Work progressing. Weather changeable. Leave to U.K. - No 29022 L/Cpl SAVAGE R.	

Army Form C. 2118.

WAR DIARY
or
INTELLIGENCE SUMMARY.
(Erase heading not required.)

Instructions regarding War Diaries and Intelligence Summaries are contained in F.S. Regs., Part II. and the Staff Manual respectively. Title pages will be prepared in manuscript.

Place	Date	Hour	Summary of Events and Information	Remarks and references to Appendices
GONNELIEU & VILLER GUISLAIN	13/8/17	-	Enemy quiet. All available men set on working party to GONNELIEU. Night quiet. Weather: rainy. From hospital :- Pte LAWSON H No 56897. Leave to U.K. :- No 17603 L/Cpl PUDDIPHAT E.	
	14/8/17		Enemy very quiet. Work on gun emplacements in GONNELIEU & shelters in the BROWN LINE progressing. Weather changeable. From hospital :- No 27699 Cpl DALY J., No 31490 Pte FENSOME G. Leave to U.K. :- No 8677 Pte JONES W.	
	15/8/17		Enemy quiet. 21st Bat. Middlesex Regt. received enemy's standing M.G.'s unmolested by firing on known hostile M-S. positions. Alternate emplacement for M.G.'s completed. Weather changeable. Deceased :- No 14633 Pte BEWSEY.C. (attached from 20th MIDDLESEX Regt.) transferred to Pin Battalion. Invalided :- No 42073 Pte FITZ-HARRIS.T from 20th MIDDLESEX Regt. attached, to replace No 14633 Pte BEWSEY.C.	
	16/8/17		Enemy quiet. Divisional Artillery concentration on enemy trenches at 10.45 p.m. & 11.45 p.m. Internal relief carried out. To hospital :- No 109 38 Cpl KILLENDER.T. Weather changeable.	

Army Form C. 2118.

WAR DIARY
OR
INTELLIGENCE SUMMARY.
(Erase heading not required.)

Instructions regarding War Diaries and Intelligence Summaries are contained in F. S. Regs., Part II. and the Staff Manual respectively. Title pages will be prepared in manuscript.

Place	Date	Hour	Summary of Events and Information	Remarks and references to Appendices
GONNELIEU & VILLERS GUISLAIN	17.8.17		Artillery active at 2.30 a.m on the left. O.C. Coy attended a Gas Course at Drummond Sur Selars FINS. Stokes & German aerial activity during the day. Anti-Aircraft armaments built by Sims in the GREEN LINE. Night firing carried out on suspected hostile Machine Gun Junctions. Weather fine.	
	18.8.17		Artillery bombardment all day in front of 8th Division on our right. New shelters for men in GREEN LINE under construction. M Gs fired bursts in co-operation with Artillery during raid on enemy's line by the 12th R.W. YORKS. Regt. Weather changeable.	
	19.8.17		Artillery bombardment at 4.30 a.m. our division away to the right. Aircraft on both sides active during the day. Weather fine. To hospital - No 63056 Pte LINTOTT W J. No 29042 Pte LAMBERT J.	
	20.8.17		Enemy quiet during the day. Artillery active on the right during the night. Weather fine. Positions selected & plans made for marking to a raid by the Division on our right. Search made for enemy Infantry Officers believed in GERMAN lines. Guns at L1. L2. L3 - M.G. 8 laid on alternate lines, GERMAN raid to be expected. 8 Guns & 119 M.G. Coy brought up to strength then expected. Weather fine.	
	21.8.17		To hospital :- No 24691 Pte HEDGES A.	

A 5834 Wt. W 4973/M 687 750,000 8/16 D. D. & L. Ltd. Forms/C. 2118/13.

WAR DIARY or INTELLIGENCE SUMMARY

Army Form C. 2118.

(Erase heading not required.)

Instructions regarding War Diaries and Intelligence Summaries are contained in F. S. Regs., Part II. and the Staff Manual respectively. Title pages will be prepared in manuscript.

Place	Date	Hour	Summary of Events and Information	Remarks and references to Appendices
GONNELIEU & VILLER GUISLAIN	22.8.17		Orders for the evening raid cancelled. Enemy raid anticipated. 4 guns of 121 Inf. Bgn & 6 guns 119 M.G. Coy fired slow 1 minute concentration with the Artillery during the night. Weather fine. To hospital:— No 29028 Sergt MONTGOMERY. J.	
"	23.8.17		Enemy cut our wire in front of NEWTON'S POST. 4 guns of 119" M.G. Coy in retaliation. Enemy raid cancelled out. Weather fine. From leave to U.K. No 70176 Pte WOODWARD W., No 33227 Pte PARMENTER B.E., No 304165 Pte COLE H.	
"	24.8.17		Enemy heavily shelled support line in front of VILLERS GUISLAIN. One casualty for four out of rations by a fragment of shell. Weather changeable.	
"	25.8.17		Enemy after shelled Support line in front of VILLERS GUISLAIN. Our Artillery retaliated. Enemy heavily shelled our QUARRY TRENCH & BLEAK SUPPORT. Night firing carried out in QUARRY TRENCH & BLEAK SUPPORT. Weather fine. To hospital:— No 63056 Pte LINTOTT W.J. No 62106 Pte BLACKWELL H. From Cambrai:— No 3741 Sergt GREEN T. from M.G. School CAMIERS.	
"	26.8.17		Enemy quiet. No work. Shells in GREEN LINE commenced. Weather changeable. On leave to U.K. No 265696 Pte DAVIS W.H.	

A5834 Wt. W4973/M687 750,000 8/16 D.D. & L. Ltd. Forms/C.2118/13.

Army Form C. 2118.

WAR DIARY
or
INTELLIGENCE SUMMARY.
(Erase heading not required.)

121st M.G. Coy

Place	Date	Hour	Summary of Events and Information	Remarks and references to Appendices
GONNELIEU – VILLER GUISLAIN	27.8.17		Enemy quiet. Works on amunit. dumps – GREEN LINE progressing. Weather raining. To hospital:– No 99744 Pte AUSTIN J.R. No 29011 Sergt McCARTHY M, No 29039 L/Cpl TREANOR F, No 21690 Pte JAMES W & No 29050 Pte CAVANAGH J. From leave to U.K.:– No 17603 L/Cpl PUDDIPHAT E.	
"	28.8.17		O.C. Coy visited G.O.C. at Bde. H.Q. Enemy not safe in our own wire; two machine guns laid in Sap during the night & M.G.8 laid on S.I. alternate S.O.S. line. Weather cloudy, strong winds. To hospital:– No 25710 Pte TAYLOR G.H. & No 53479 Pte CROOK A.	
	29.8.17		Hostile artillery very lively around TURNERS QUARRY. Night from changed over "A" (GREEN) & "BROWN" LINES relieved the teams – Mg 3 M 47, M 58 M 99 & L.C.L.2. Weather wet. From hospital:– Pte WILDING J.H. From leave to U.K.:– Pte JONES W. To camp:– No 32471 Dr GANT W. Farriery Course ABBEVILLE	
	30.8.17		Enemy quiet. Works. The line progressing. Weather showery. From hospital:– 2nd Lt THORPE T. + On boat No 29031 Pte ARMSTRONG D.P. 2nd/Lieut BANKS & Gunner No 87691 Pte JACKSON A. From hospital:– C.S.M. LUCK F No 54823. On Course:–	

A5834 Wt.W4973/M687 750,000 8/16 D.D.&L. Ltd. Forms/C.2118/13.

WAR DIARY
or
INTELLIGENCE SUMMARY.

(Erase heading not required.)

Army Form C. 2118.

Place	Date	Hour	Summary of Events and Information	Remarks and references to Appendices
GONNELIEU - VILLERS GUISLAIN	31.8.17		O.C. Coy attended G.O.C.'s conference. At 4.15 a.m. enemy rushed our line near TURNER'S QUARRY. Machine guns put down a barrage. MG5 MG7 MG8 L1 L2 L3. MG2 MG3 R1 fired in the S.O.S. lines. MG9 fired on M/G activate S.O.S. line. No firing carried out. Weather changeable. Strength returns:- Auth'd RANKS A.U.K. Auth'y 3rd Army A/D/11/1 3rd Corps A/V/27/7 H.D. 10 Div 120 A No 27/00 P.C. ROCHE C.R. & BASE Auth'y G.H.Q. A/6869.	

Mathieson Major
Commanding 121 Coy M.G. Corps

In the field
31/8/17

Army Form C. 2118.

WAR DIARY
or
INTELLIGENCE SUMMARY.
(Erase heading not required.)

Instructions regarding War Diaries and Intelligence Summaries are contained in F. S. Regs., Part II. and the Staff Manual respectively. Title pages will be prepared in manuscript.

Place	Date	Hour	Summary of Events and Information	Remarks and references to Appendices
			Casualties	
			Killed Wounded Admitted to hospital	
			Officers 1	
			N.C.Os 4	
			Men 13	
			Reinforcements	
			Officers 1	
			N.C.Os -	
			Men 3 Total for month 4	
			Total for month 18	
			Attached from Battalions 15 men.	
			Ammunition fired etc.	
			Number of guns fired during month 64	
			S.A.A. expended 129,550	
			Number of targets engaged 50. Average number of rounds fired by a gun in one night	
				20,00
			In the field	
			31/8/17	

Mathison Major
Commanding 121 M.G. Coy.

Confidential.

Original.
Vol 16

War Diary

– of –

121st Company Machine Gun Corps

From 1st September 1917 To 30th September 1917.

Volumn 15

WAR DIARY
or
INTELLIGENCE SUMMARY.
(Erase heading not required.)

Army Form C. 2118.

Instructions regarding War Diaries and Intelligence Summaries are contained in F. S. Regs., Part II. and the Staff Manual respectively. Title pages will be prepared in manuscript.

Place	Date	Hour	Summary of Events and Information	Remarks and references to Appendices
GONNELIEU & VILLERS GUISLAIN	1.9.17		Enemy artillery active. Day firing canalised over front line trenches. Wounded — Nº 29028 Sergt MONTGOMERY + Nº 83730 Pte JOHNSON W.H.	
	2.9.17		10 & R gun positions nearer to deliver the junction of HIGH ST + GEORGIE ST. Work commenced on new gun positions. Hostile & friendly artillery active. Weather — changeable. Wounded — Nº 63106 Pte BLACKWELL H. From shell fire. — Near BAIN A.M.R., Nº 29006 Pte HORAN A. Nº 29034 Pte BRYSON T. (Malta) (Both officers) to Hospital.	FIFE ROAD & HIGH ST.
	3.9.17		Enemy artillery active. Guns & positions L1, L2 M.G's fired on targets in the vicinity of the junction of during the night. Enemy bombing carried out in co-operation with the artillery. Withdrawal having failed. Reinforcements:— Nº 204) Pte KNOWLES J.W. attached from 2nd MIDDLESEX REGT.	
	4.9.17		Enemy very quiet. L1 L2 M.G. again fired on normal S.O.S. lines. Artillery firing canalised out. Hostile firing. Reinforcements Nº 29691 Pte NEDGES A. Shylift clemence:— Nº 88206 Pte COOK R + Nº 12706 Pte JOHNSON J to M.G.C. Base.	

Army Form C. 2118.

WAR DIARY
or
INTELLIGENCE SUMMARY.

(Erase heading not required.)

Instructions regarding War Diaries and Intelligence Summaries are contained in F. S. Regs., Part II. and the Staff Manual respectively. Title pages will be prepared in manuscript.

Place	Date	Hour	Summary of Events and Information	Remarks and references to Appendices
GONNELIEUT VILLERS GUISLAIN	5-9-17		Enemy artillery active during the day. Consideration fired during the night by our artillery on machine guns. Weather fine. To hospital:- Lieut WANN S.A. & No 25715 Pte GREEN S.J. (both M.G. Rifle Officer). Slightly wounded:- No 18819 Pte GLOVER A attached from 21st Bn MIDDLESEX Regt returned to his unit. To U.K.:- Hon. Lieut. PIERCE M. No 29009.	
	6-9-17		Enemy quiet. Nothing of the importance. No attack or transport heard on all constitution. Weather fine. At Rest:- CHAPMAN G.P. at U.K. authority A.G. No A/2297/70.	
	7-9-17		Enemy inquietud in due in the vicinity of HIGH STREET. night fighting carried out in co-operation our artillery as enemy were likely to assemble for a raid. Weather fine. Reinforcements:- No 54906 Pte ILES C.J. from Base. From hospital:- No 8477 Pte JONES W. & No 83479 Pte CROOK.A. To hospital:- No 64717 Pte RUST K & No 64286 Pte WYLIE W. Leave to U.K.:- 2nd Lieut ELLIS E.	
	8-9-17		Enemy quiet. Great aerial activity. 12th Bn YORKSHIRE REGT carried out a raid during which materials from front in unofficial battly in functions. Weather fine. From hospital:- Lieut WANN S.A. & No 25715 Pte GREEN S.J. (both ---) To hospital:- No 29437 Pte CALOW S. (attached from 11th YORKSHIRE REGT) From leave to U.K.:- No 25696 Pte DAVIES W.M. & No 28950 Pte CAVANAGH T.	

Army Form C. 2118.

WAR DIARY
or
INTELLIGENCE SUMMARY.
(Erase heading not required.)

Instructions regarding War Diaries and Intelligence Summaries are contained in F. S. Regs., Part II. and the Staff Manual respectively. Title pages will be prepared in manuscript.

Place	Date	Hour	Summary of Events and Information	Remarks and references to Appendices
GONNELIEU VILLERS GUISLAIN	9.9.17		Present turn shelled by enemy Artillery	
	10.9.17		Armed activity on both sides	
	10.9.17		Work in the trenches. Weather fine	
			Everything quiet. Shelter at M.G. & Lewis gun team completed. Night from. Carried out from leave to U.K. :- No 29039 L/cpl TREANOR F. & No 24690 Pte JAMES W. Weather fine.	
	11.9.17		Everything quiet. Weather fine. Positions chosen for New Claymore Sniping gun + position connected to O P by telephone. Reinforcements :- No 105334 L/cpl SMITH E.W. No 89750 Pte JOHNSON W.H. To hospital :- No 2901 Sgt McCARTHY M. From leave to U.K. :-	
	12.9.17		Everything quiet. Day front. Carried out with sniping guns. Night front. Carried out in co-operation with the Artillery. To hospital :- No 63923 Pte BEAUMONT W. Leave to U.K. :- No 24697 Pte KINSELLA J. Weather fine	
	13.9.17		Everything quiet during the day. Daylight carried out by sniping guns. Night firing carried out in co-operation with Artillery & Trench Mortars. Weather :- Changeable. Leave to U.K. No 25585 Pte CAIRNS W. (attd. Batn. A attached C.S.)	

A5834 Wt.W4973/M687 750,000 8/16 D.D.&L.Ltd. Forms/C.2118/13.

Army Form C. 2118.

WAR DIARY
or
INTELLIGENCE SUMMARY.
(Erase heading not required.)

Instructions regarding War Diaries and Intelligence Summaries are contained in F. S. Regs., Part II. and the Staff Manual respectively. Title pages will be prepared in manuscript.

Place	Date	Hour	Summary of Events and Information	Remarks and references to Appendices
GONNELIEU & VILLERS GUISLAIN	14.9.17		Enemy quiet during the day. Day & night carried out our sniping game. Night carried out in co-operation with Artillery as well in the usual nightly firing & harassing. Weather changeable.	
	15.9.17		Everything quiet. Day & night carried out by sniping game. Work at our Headquarters. Losses O.R. :- No. 25706 Pte HOBBS T.B. From Rest Camp :- No. 14360 Pte CRAWFORD T. & No. 29005 Pte LESTRANGE. E.	
	16.9.17		Position of enemy gun on left moved to new position at R.24.6.30.10. 1st Brigade on our right raided hostile enemy trenches, while our machine guns fired in HUNNECOURT WOOD & avoided 100 m.g. try to put up a barrage round the objective in Number trenches. Enemy quiet, nightly firing & harassing.	
	17.9.17		Nightly firing carried out in co-operation with the Artillery in trenches in R.29.a. & assistance for a group of 3 guns situated off KITCHIN ROAD. Weather fine. Rain occasionally. No. 63683 Pte WRIGHT. W. No. 63635 Pte KIRKHAM C.H.	

Report on Operations

on the night of 5th/6th May 1917

— at —

LA VACQUERIE

P. Mathison. Major
O.C. 121 MACHINE GUN COMPANY
121 INFANTRY BRIGADE
IN THE FIELD

DATE 9th May 1917

Army Form C. 2118.

WAR DIARY
or
INTELLIGENCE SUMMARY.
(Erase heading not required.)

Instructions regarding War Diaries and Intelligence Summaries are contained in F. S. Regs., Part II. and the Staff Manual respectively. Title pages will be prepared in manuscript.

Place	Date	Hour	Summary of Events and Information	Remarks and references to Appendices
GONNELIEU & VILLERS GUISLAIN	18.9.17		Heavy guns. Day firing carried out by enemy guns, two direct hits obtained. Position reported off HIGH STREET for a group of 3 guns. Weather fine. Ham Duffers :- No 63923 Pte BEAUMONT.W. Shingle dismissed. 1st O.R. attached from Battalions returned to their units	
"	19.9.17		Day firing turned out by enemy guns, one direct hit obtained. Position for a group of 3 guns reported off CHESHIRE STREET. Dinner plans dropped down by hostile A.A. shells in RO RAVINE. Near position of batteries KITCHIN ROAD commenced. Weather fine.	
"	20.9.17		Enemy firing quiet. Work on all positions continued. Night firing carried out. Weather fine. To Hospital :- No 29034 Pte BRYSON. T	
"	21.9.17		Enemy firing quiet. Work on new positions progressing and R.E. available. Night firing carried out. Weather fine. To Hospital :- No 18427. C.Q.M.Serjt SMITH. T.R. Dismissed :- No 52460 Pte WALTON. H No 52614 Pte WOODAGE. W. } 1st Divisional Signal School NURLU No 67842 Pte WEST. N. No 29008 Pte DOWLING. J. From leave to U.K. - 2nd Lieut ELLIS. T.E.	

WAR DIARY
or
INTELLIGENCE SUMMARY.

Army Form C. 2118.

Place	Date	Hour	Summary of Events and Information	Remarks and references to Appendices
GONNELIEU & VILLERS GUISLAIN	22.9.17		O.C. Coy. attended a Conference with C.R.A. at Divisional H.Q. At dusk the 120 Bde. on our left made a successful raid on the enemy's line. Casualties from gun fire:- No. 25710 Pte. TAYLOR C.H. Slightly Bruised. No. 15427 P.S. Sergt. SMITH I.R. to C.C.S.	
"	23.9.17		Enemy's Artillery active. Special hostile artillery on both sides. Nil for enemy. Casualties:- No. 6428 Pte. WYLIE W. Slightly shaken :- No. 29744 Pte. AUSTIN J.R. to C.C.S. From hospital. No. 29009 L/Cpl. PIERCE M. from leave.	
"	24.9.17		Artillery on both sides active. Special precautions taken against hostile aircraft. Officers of 244 M.G. Coy reconnoitred the areas allotted to them for gun positions during the coming relief. From leave :- Pte. KINSELLA J. No. 29697. Sergt. ORR H. No. 29701.	
"	25.9.17		All machine gun mounted in forward positions fired during the day, nice firing during the raid, by German our artillery bombarded enemy's trenches 3 mile round and were afterwards shelled with 5.9 for anti aircraft went during the day. 4 machine guns afterwards reted. At 7.30 p.m. 10th Batt SUFFOLK REGT raided the enemy trenches. 22 machine guns put up a barrage around the vicinity of the objective. 4 machine guns were kept in reserve. To hospital:- No. 9748 Pte. THORPE C.H. Wounded remained on duty :- Lieut. NALE A.P. & No. 29019 L/Cpl. TREANOR. From leave :- U.K. No. 25715 Pte. GREEN S.J.	
VILLERS GUISLAIN	26.9.17		Machine guns fired at aircraft. Enemy Artillery during the day. Machine gun fired on areas damaged by the relief on advances during the day & night. New m.g. positions reconnoitred. Reinforcements :- No. 53423 Pte. HAINES W.J. & No. 3.0725 Pte. HALL 14. From hospital :- No. 29012 Pte. QUALEY J.	

A 5834 Wt.W4973/M687 750,000 8/16 D.D.&L.Ltd. Forms/C.2118/13.

WAR DIARY or INTELLIGENCE SUMMARY

Army Form C. 2118.

Place	Date	Hour	Summary of Events and Information	Remarks and references to Appendices
GONNELIEU	27.9.17		Everything quiet. Sniping guns obtain a bit. Went on new munition programme. Weather fine. Enquiry from Horse Command No 29701 Sergt ORR H. Wounded — No 29017 Pte Bagley C. to hospital.	
VILLERS GUISLAIN	28.9.17		Everything quiet. Night firing carried out in co-operation with the Artillery. Weather fine. From Reserve — No 253585 P.G. CAIRNS W. (attached).	
	29.9.17		Everything quiet. Night firing carried out in co-operation with the Artillery, & also on targets in the area damaged by the raid on the 25th. Weather fine. On Command — LIEUT A.P. MALE. No 30165 P.G. COLE H. (Batman) No 27690 Sergt BRENNAN C. No 29722 Sergt SLACKE R.H. M.G. Corps CAMIERS.	
	30.9.17		Enemy Artillery active during the day. Amt activity on both sides. 2nd Coy Machine Gun Corps relieved 121st Coy Machine Gun Corps in the "GONNELIEU" & VILLERS GUISLAIN Sectors. On being relieved 121st Coy M.G.C. proceeded to HEUDECOURT in Divisional Reserve.	

In the field
30/9/17

P. Mathieson Major
Commanding 121st Coy. M.G. Corps

SECRET.   Copy No. 1.

OPERATION ORDERS
BY
MAJOR. P. MATHISEN.
Commanding 121st Company MACHINE GUN CORPS.

22nd September 1917.

Ref. Special Sheet Ed. 1.
GOUZEAUCOURT 1/20,000

1. **General Scheme**

    Raid will be carried out on night 25th/26th September on Enemy's Trenches in R.28.d.

    Objects.

    (I.) Obtain Prisoners identifications and material.

    (II.) Destroy dug-outs material and defences.

2. **Machine Guns.**

    The 121st. Company Machine Gun Corps in co-operation with 119th Company Machine Gun Corps and 244th Company Machine Gun Corps divided into 8 Groups in all 26 Guns will put up a Box Barrage around vicinity of objective. The whole to be under Orders of O.C. 121st. Company Machine Gun Corps.

3. **Reconnaisance.**

    Officers commanding Groups will select actual Gun Positions in the areas allotted to engage Targets as follows:-

Group	No. of Guns.	Approximate Gun Position.	Target.
1.	4.	R.20 d. 50.30.	From R.28 a. 75.55. to R.28 b. 65.20.
2.	4.	R.20 d. 30.15.	" R.28 b. 35.20 to R.29 c. 20.70.
3.	2.	R.32 b. 30.10.	" BLEAK WALK (R.28 a. 50.05 to R.28 a. 90.25)
4.	4.	R.33 a. 10.40.	" QUARRY SUPPORT at R.29 c. 20.70 to R.29 c. 90.95.
5.	4.	R.33 a. 50.10.	" QUARRY TRENCH (R.29 c. 25.40 to R.29 d. 20.60.)
6.	2.	X.4 c. 35.65.	" R.29 c. 45.70. to R.28 a. 50.05.
7.	2.	X.4 d. 60.75.	" R.29 c. 30.35 to R.29 c. 25.80.
8.	4.	X.3 a. 55.90.	Reserve Guns on S.O.S. Lines.

Number 8 Group will take up A.A. positions in DUMP COPSE. X 3 a. 50. 70. These Guns to be used for Anti-Aircraft work from 7 A.M. until 30 minutes before ZERO when they will move forward and occupy Battle Positions in Reserve Trench. Reserve Guns to be under Orders of C.O. 12th. Battalion Suffolk Regiment.

4. <u>Time of Firing</u>

Machine Guns will open fire at ZERO + 3 to ZERO + 70. Barrage will then cease unless otherwise ordered.

5. <u>Night Lines</u> will be carefully laid out, actual Gun Positions pegged and pegs put out for Night Firing Boxes. Compasses to be checked and variation carefully noted.

6. <u>Emplacements</u> to be constructed. Lines laid out. Ammunition supply and everything completed by morning of 24th/25th inst.

7. <u>Laying of Guns</u>.

All Guns to be in position and laid by dusk by Officers. Clinometers to be used and when completed reports to that effect to be wired in Code to Company Headquarters. Code word to be used "IN."

8. <u>Communications</u>.

All reports and messages to Company Headquarters. 2 Orderlies to be with each Group and 1 Orderly for each Group to be at Advanced Company Headquarters. Urgent messages by Wire from nearest Infantry Company Headquarters. Reserve Guns to be in Telephonic communication with Advanced Headquarters 12th. Bn. Suffolk Regiment.

9. <u>Medical Arrangements</u>.

Advanced Dressing Station CHESHIRE QUARRY
Aid Post at R 26 d. 70.05.
Dressing Station at X 3 d. 00.10.

10. <u>Watches to be Synchronised</u> at Headquarters Right Group Artillery four hours before ZERO and to be checked by Wire two hours before ZERO.

11. <u>ZERO</u> to be notified later.

12. <u>Company Headquarters</u> will remain at present location.

13. <u>Transport</u> will take all Belts, Screens, S.A.A. Water etc. on to the Gun Positions. After Limbers have been emptied they will proceed to selected positions under cover and await further Orders.

14. <u>Reports</u> to be forwarded to the Advanced Company Headquarters after the Operation giving full details.

15. <u>Gas</u>
Every precaution to be taken against Hostile Gas Shells.

16. <u>Acknowledge.</u>

Nº 1, 2 & 3.	War Diary.
4.	Office
5, 6, 7, 8, 9, 10, 11, 12.	Group Commanders
13, 14, 15, 16.	Battalions.
17.	T.M.B.
18.	Brigade
19.	D.M.G.O.
20.	Transport Officer
21.	M.A.P.
22.	O.C. 119 Company
23.	O.C. 244. Company.

Mathison MAJOR
Commanding 121st. Company
MACHINE GUN CORPS.

SECRET.

Copy No. 1.

OPERATION ORDERS

— BY —

MAJOR P. MATHISON

Commanding 121st Company MACHINE GUN CORPS.

PART II

1. **Points Before and During Firing** will be carefully attended to.

2. **Ammunition Supply**
   Each Gun will have 10 full Belt Boxes at Gun Position.

3. **Control**
   Each sub-section (2 Guns) to be controlled by an Officer.

4. **Rate of Fire**
   150 Rounds per minute. Care to be taken to ensure that this is not exceeded.

5. **Laying of Fire**
   After every burst aim will be checked on Night Firing Box and elevation checked after every 1,000 rounds by Clinometer. Every chance will be taken to fill up and check water.

6. **Oil and Water**
   A supply of each to be kept on Gun Positions.

7. **Screens** will be used to conceal flash.

   Condenser and Bag to be used.

9. <u>Instruments to be used.</u>

   Liquid Compass, Clinometers, Abney Levels, Directors.

10. <u>Night Firing Boxes</u> to be overhauled

11. All empty cases to be collected and returned to Quartermaster's Stores.

APPENDIX. I

12. Map showing Barrage Lines and Disposition of Guns attached

Date: 22nd September 1917.

P. Mathison
MAJOR
Commanding 121st Company
MACHINE GUN CORPS.

Issued to :-
   Diary
   O.C. 119th Company
   O.C. 244th Company
   Office
   Group Commanders.

BARRAGE MAP   APPENDIX I

Army Form C. 2118.

WAR DIARY
or
INTELLIGENCE SUMMARY.
(Erase heading not required.)

Instructions regarding War Diaries and Intelligence Summaries are contained in F. S. Regs., Part II. and the Staff Manual respectively. Title pages will be prepared in manuscript.

Place	Date	Hour	Summary of Events and Information	Remarks and references to Appendices
			Casualties. Wounded. Admitted to hospital.	
			Officers — 2	
			N.C.O.s — 1	
			Men — 9	
			Total for month. 14	
			Reinforcements.	
			Officers — 1	
			N.C.O.s — —	
			Men — 6	
			Total for month. 7 O.R.	
			Indented for.	
			Number of Guns fired during month. 109	
			S.A.A. expended. 340,000 rounds.	
			Number of targets engaged. 246.	

In the Field
30/9/17

@ Matheson Major.
Commanding 121 M.G. Coy

Original

Confidential.

Vol 17

War Diary
—of—
Machine Gun Corps

121st Company

From 1st October 1917 To 31st October 1917

Volumn 16

WAR DIARY
or
INTELLIGENCE SUMMARY.
(Erase heading not required.)

Army Form C. 2118.

Place	Date	Hour	Summary of Events and Information	Remarks and references to Appendices
HEUDICOURT	1.10.17		Day spent in cleaning up after being relieved in the GONNELIEU VILLERS GUISLAIN Sector. Hostile fire. To Divisional — No 62365 Pte LOWERY G. LAVRE & LE HAVRE — Lieut A H VILLIERS	
"	2.10.17		Training commenced. Hostile fire. To Divisional No 85347 Pte MOORE W. No 63100 Pte BLACKWELL H (no information to rank officer)	
"	3.10.17		Day spent in training. No 2 Section under Lieut ROBINSON returned a received (24 hrs) by M.G.C. to the VILLERS GUISLAIN Sector. Gun transferred No 19491 Pte THORPE. C.H.	
"	4.10.17		Salvaging continued. 2nd Lt HULL & 2nd Lt ELLIS & 2nd Lt THORPE received instructions. Guns to the GONNELIEU sector for firing operations of 141 Brigade. 12 Guns sent. Arrived at the line at dawn & moved up to allotted position. Heavy fall mist throughout.	
"	5.10.17		Enemy & Rear harassed aircraft MG fire. Sgt H ½. Hostile — Reel returned ACH H.Q. No 31691 Pte FANTHAM A Reels 31 operated. Nos 1 & 2 Sections front line No 3242 Pte BAILEY. B Reinforcements. PG HOBBS T.B. 3 men Commission: N 34160 Pte WEST W.M. No 47242 Pte DOWLING T No 34544 Pte WOODAGE H. No 26083 Pte DOWLING T	

Army Form C. 2118.

WAR DIARY
or
INTELLIGENCE SUMMARY.
(Erase heading not required.)

Instructions regarding War Diaries and Intelligence Summaries are contained in F. S. Regs., Part II. and the Staff Manual respectively. Title pages will be prepared in manuscript.

Place	Date	Hour	Summary of Events and Information	Remarks and references to Appendices
HEUDICOURT	6.10.17		No 2 Section relieved by No 1 Section in VILLERS GUISLAIN Sector. Weather wet.	
"	7.10.17		Hour Rapports. No 32250 Pte STEAD B. No 09903 Pte WRIGHT R. Man attended Church Parade, remainder of day spent in training. Weather fair. From leave to LE HAVRE - Lieut A.H. VILLIERS	
"	8.10.17		Day spent in training. Weather wet. From hospital No 52365 Pte LOWERY G, No 25702 Pte GOSSIN R & No 29002 Pte DUWLING J. To hospital No 29990 Pte CROSS A.H.	
"	9.10.17		Day spent in training. Weather fair. No 1 Section relieved in VILLERS GUISLAIN Sector & now attached to LIEREN? To hospital - No 62990 Pte CROSS A.H.	
"	10.10.17		Company proceeded to PERONNE by DECAUVILLE Railway, remained in PERONNE the night. Strength strenuous?: On leave to U.K. - No 32250 Pte B STEAD from leave U.K. No 869024 Pte GREEN J.	
PERONNE	11.10.17		Day spent in Billets in PERONNE. Weather wet. To hospital - No 67842 Pte WEST C.N., No 70376 Pte WOODWARD W., No 28909 L/Cpl WATTERS J.	

Army Form C. 2118.

WAR DIARY
or
INTELLIGENCE SUMMARY.
(Erase heading not required.)

Instructions regarding War Diaries and Intelligence Summaries are contained in F. S. Regs., Part II. and the Staff Manual respectively. Title pages will be prepared in manuscript.

Place	Date	Hour	Summary of Events and Information	Remarks and references to Appendices
PERONNE.	12.10.17		The Company entrained at PERONNE during the morning & detrained at BEAUMETZ at 10 P.M.	BEAUMETZ-LES-LOGES
			The Company arrived at LA HERLIERE at midnight & occupied huts to the rear in the offices in farms.	
LA HERLIERE	13.10.17		Day spent in cleaning up & improving huts. Training commenced. Weather fair. On inwards – No. 3741 C.S.M. GREEN to UK returned 1st Bn 4th Bn DIV No. 90/4D & 91 No. 31/573/403.	
"	15.10.17		Day spent in training. 4 officers proceeded to DOULLENS for the day. Weather changeable.	
"	16.10.17		Day spent in training. O.C. Coy attended Brigade Conference. Weather fine.	
"	17.10.17		Day spent in training. Morning spent in instructing the Company. The Company paraded for a route march in the afternoon. Weather fine.	
"	19.10.17		Day spent in training. Sergt K. BERNARD – No. 4413 Pte FISHKIN F & others returned as unfit reserve.	

A5834 Wt. W4973/M687 750,000 8/16 D.D. & L. Ltd. Forms/C.2118/13.

Army Form C. 2118.

WAR DIARY
or
INTELLIGENCE SUMMARY.
(Erase heading not required.)

Place	Date	Hour	Summary of Events and Information	Remarks and references to Appendices
LAHERLERE	20.10.17		Day spent in the usual Brig. Point Talks & Sir nov parades in full marching order carrying packs & blankets for inspection by G.O.C. Bde.	
			Trans W.V.K. No 30413 A/CPL ELLIOT F. Weather fine	
	21.10.17		G.O.C. Brigade inspected the Bn jobs. After the inspection the company marched to Church parade. Weather fine.	
			To not Comtt — No 29035 Pte Cameron J. No 29046 Pte Pleasance T. No 24747 Pte Root F.A. No 29705 Pte Wade J.	
	22.10.17		One Cay ban G.O.C. Brigade inaugurated the formation of a Battalion school on 24.10.17	
			Ref [illeg] No 29011 Sgt McCarthy M. from hospital has been found.	
			Day spent training. Salvage Officers manning the ground for the benefit for Ball Balkes	
			Reinforcements:— No 51128 Pte Sawyer C.E.	
			Good promoted:— No 6471 Pte Rust K. No 47892 Pte West C.H.	
			To hospital:— No 29030 Pte Cavanagh T. No 29261 Pte George W.H. & Robert (leading) Gunner	
	24.10.17		Tactical Scheme "Ball & Whistle" the whole Brigade taking part. Weather fine.	
			To hospital No 20164 Pte Ford F. Sgt & Survines No 81030 Pte Cavanagh J. discharged to C.C.S	

A5834 Wt. W4973/M687 750,000 8/16 D. D. & L. Ltd. Forms/C.2118/13.

Army Form C. 2118.

WAR DIARY
or
INTELLIGENCE SUMMARY.
(Erase heading not required.)

Instructions regarding War Diaries and Intelligence Summaries are contained in F. S. Regs., Part II. and the Staff Manual respectively. Title pages will be prepared in manuscript.

Place	Date	Hour	Summary of Events and Information	Remarks and references to Appendices
LA HERLIÈRE	25.10.17		Day spent in training in the camp. Troops were inspected by G.O.C. Brigade. Weather changeable from this p.m. Shortly afterwards No 29905 Pte DOWLING I., No 25702 Pte GOGGIN R. from Bases A.V.K. No 30164 Pte FURDIE from Bases A.V.K. No 32950 Pte STEAD B.	
	26.10.17		Day spent in training. Weather N.W. From this pitch A.M.R. RAIN M.C., No 68306 Pte BLACKWELL H. (A.V.K) No 97694 Pte WITHERS R.	
	27.10.17		Tactical scheme of 24.10.17. completed. Weather fair. Reinforcements- No 53776 Cpl G.M. Smith BETT R. from 6 Aug M.G.C No 14818 Pte SAMUELS J.	
	28.10.17		Runners & Scouts in the evening. Remainder of men off duty apart in preparing to meet Lieut VILLIERS who acted as visiting officer	
	29.10.17		The Company moved by march from LA HERLIÈRE to GOMIECOURT during the morning afternoon. At GOMIECOURT Bn HQrs was visited by MAJOR R. MATHIESON on leave A.V.K. LIEUT E.G. HERBERT assumed command of the Company	

A5834 Wt. W4973/M687 750,000 8/16 D. D. & L. Ltd. Forms/C.2113/13.

WAR DIARY
or
INTELLIGENCE SUMMARY.
(Erase heading not required.)

Army Form C. 2118.

Place	Date	Hour	Summary of Events and Information	Remarks and references to Appendices
SOMBRIN	30/10/17	—	Day spent in leaving the Company in Bowange Drive. Weather changeable. Reinforcements. — No 116304 Pte OSOSKI D & No 116206 Pte SOWERBY H. Sent hospital. — No 29506 Pte HORAN A. Courses. — hui. A.P. MALE. & No 30966 Pte COLE H. (Lectures) No 27690 Sergt BRENNAN C. No 29703 Sergt SLACK R.H. No 29361 Pte PEARCE W.H.	
"	31/10/17	—	Day spent in training the Company in Barrage Drill & recreational Game. Weather fine. O.C. Coy attended conference at Brigade H.Q. From next camp. — No 29032 Pte CURRAN J. No 29096 Pte PLEASANCE T No 26570 Pte RUST F.A. & No 27705 Pte WADE J.	

In the Field
31/10/17

Kandein(?)
O.C. 121st Company
Machine Gun Corps

Confidential

Vol 18

War Diary
of
121st Company Machine Guns Corps

From 1st November 1917 to 30 November 1917

Volume 17

WAR DIARY or INTELLIGENCE SUMMARY

Army Form C. 2118.

Pelmot 121 Infantry
107th Infantry Brigade 16/5/61

Place	Date	Hour	Summary of Events and Information	Remarks and references to Appendices
SCHOBERN	1.11.17		Bay short & Evening. Battalion att was a tactical exercise with the	
			12" Bn Yorkshire Regt.	
			Reinforcement. No.10485 Corp. KILLENDER. J.	
			Sergt. M Donovan No 3741 L/Sergt. GREEN Q.U.R.	
			Private Q.U.K. No 48240 Pte LAWRENCE. R.	
		2.11.17	Bay Shoot & Training. Wheeler Jas.	
			Bay short & Training.	
			York Fusilers No 62488 Pte CROSSAN	
		3.11.17	Reinf Q.U.R RIDRGT CL TIERNEY L No 25702 Pte GOGGIN R	
			After Noon Q.U.R 2/Lt ELLIOTT F	
		4.11.17	Bay shoot & Training	
			Inniscours No 34533 Pte ARMAGHER E V Sanitary Sgt St POLLS	
			Reinft Q.U.R. 22.971 Pte WARD H L. No 31489 Pte FLETCHER W	
			Smyth Alterus. No 47674 Pte WITHERS R.G	
		5.11.17	Bay shoot & Training	
			L Sub. Q.U.R No 29030 Pte WRIGHT R & No 28699 Pte OAKERBEE H	

Army Form C. 2118.

WAR DIARY
or
INTELLIGENCE SUMMARY.
(Erase heading not required.)

Army Form C. 2118.

121st M.G.C.
121st M[?] Bn 48th [?]

Instructions regarding War Diaries and Intelligence Summaries are contained in F.S. Regs., Part II. and the Staff Manual respectively. Title pages will be prepared in manuscript.

Place	Date	Hour	Summary of Events and Information	Remarks and references to Appendices
SONDRIN	6/11		Day spent [in] [?] U.S. Camp out and [?] details with Hd Q's C	
			[?] H.Q. No 36050 Pte PEARMAN T, Nº 26050 Pte SMITH P.	
	Daily		Day spent in training Weather fine	
			L/Cpl S.G. DAVEY joins the Coy as O.C. carrying party	
			in command Nº 43283 Corp TRISTAN O. MC SHANE Artillery	
			Signals C.U.K. 80 25.991 Pte HEDGES A + Nº 31490 Pte FENSOME F.	
			[?] [?] Nº 9448 Pte REES T, Nº 85347 Pte MOOREW, Nº 67905 Pte CAMERON A.	
			Reinforcements Nº 348,655 Pte GARDINER G.H.	
	8.11		L/Cpl Johnson Bryceson Testing in [?]	
			Recruits U.K. Nº 24736, Pte PEARCE W.H	
			From course Nº 31523 Pte ARMIGER S.V.	
			Day still in [?] [?] to Coy are out [?] [?] ie of 13/6 H.Q	
			[?] S.G. DAVEY reported [?] [?] Sgt [?]	
			MAJOR P MATHISON [?] from [?] U.K.	
			[?] U.K. Nº 28246 Pte FAIRWAY, Nº 857.6 Pte PRYOR W.F. [?] DIGGINS HICKS E	
			[?] [?] [?] Nº [?] Pte LAMBERT J	

A6945 Wt. W11422/M1160 350,000 12/16 D. D. & L. Forms/C./2118/14.

WAR DIARY
or
INTELLIGENCE SUMMARY

Army Form C. 2118.

Place	Date	Hour	Summary of Events and Information	Remarks and references to Appendices
SCARPIN	10.11.17		Day spent in training	
			Inform return for U.K.	
			Strength decrease	
			The Revd A.W.R. Shaw, A.M.R. BAIN M.C.	
			the Revd P. MATHISEN A.R.N. returned with the company to Canaupt & Capt DARLEY	
	11.11.17		O.C. Divisional Train notified all ranks anxious to	
			Coy attend Church Parade Afternoon of a Pageant of Trans	
			Revd A.C.F. No 25710 Pte TAYLOR G.H.	
			Game Everfield - No 70376 Pte WOODWARD J.	
			Day spent as usual with exception	
	12.11.17		Revd C.U.R. No 29012 Pte COPLEY T / No 27103 Pte STEWART R.	
	13.11.17		Day spent in Training Rifles Issued Carried out from Battle by inf/or	
			and taken to training by both arrivals	
			Leave U.K. No 25688 Pte ROBERT J. (R)	
	14.11.17		Day spent in Training Afternoon Recreational Training small retire with	
			Section officer	
			Leave U.K. Pte MUGFORD No 25733. PRISONER No 29052 Pte JOSSON No STAFF KEENE

Army Form C. 2118.

WAR DIARY
or
INTELLIGENCE SUMMARY.

(Erase heading not required.)

War No IV
191st M.G.C.
191st Bde Inf. Bde

Place	Date	Hour	Summary of Events and Information	Remarks and references to Appendices
SOMBRIN	15.11.17		Lectures FIELDAY by ROBERMONT WOOD. Remainder Training in SOMBRIN. Reinforcements No 85554 Pte SHEDRICK, No 85271 Pte BROWN, No 9174 Pte WITHERS. LEAVE U.K. No 26685 Pte KEELE 'C'. 89)	
	16.11.17		Training in SOMBRIN. Brigade Rd Party Co walk for all M.G officers rendezvous with the 91e)	
AHURLIERE	17.11.17		Training in SOMBRIN. Small scheme for section officers. Company moved to AHURLIERE. To the FIELD No 27605 Pte DUCK f. No 10814 Pte WILLIAMS (No 52127 Pte HAMMET, leave EUK. No 25713 Pte FRANKLIN G. H. 'A'9)	
AHURLIERE	18.11.17		ACHIET-LE-PETIT. Company marched to AHURLIERE. Small Tactical walk with section officers. From No 85750 Pte JOHNSON to North No 27753 Pte NAGE. Pte THORPE	
ACHIET LE PETIT	19.11.17		Training, men attached from infantry as carrying party and Belle-julien Leave U.K. No 14365 Pte CRAWFORD J.	
ROCQUIGNY	20.11.17		Company moved to ROCQUIGNY. Men & Officers in MIREMONT HUT.	
	21.11.17		All surplus kit dumped to the Bois Bois Mons. BARRATRE area. Company moved to BEAUMETZ. 89)	
BEAUMETZ	22.11.17		Company under orders at BEAUMETZ, moved to RAINCOURT. Officers & Men in huts. 89)	

WAR DIARY or INTELLIGENCE SUMMARY

Army Form C. 2118.

191st M.G.Coy
191st Inf Bde
1st Div

Place	Date	Hour	Summary of Events and Information	Remarks and references to Appendices
GRAINCOURT	23.11.17	10.30am	Company attached in support of Infantry against BOURLON Wood & Village. Some guns in BOURLON Wood, 4 a SMALE Released 11.30am at ANVILLERS Railway Halt dugout at 12noon.	
		11.45am		
		4.1pm	Guns instructed to withdraw to STAR and Crown salient, left flank. Enemy attacked & 20 m officers killed & wounded. Strength reduced to 20 m officers killed & wounded at BRINSON after HULK. 6742 Pt WESTON; No.24002 Pt HOST; wounded at BRINSON after HULK. 3/Lt ELLIS, No.24266 Sgt McCARTHY, 2702 Pte KLACKE, 46573 Pte CURRY; 35742 Rqt Hosp, 35917 Pte ELLIOTT; 85289 Pte McBETH; 35526 Pte CAMERON; 35725 Pte BELL; 68166 Pte ARNSAA; 24005 Pte LaGRANGE 2579 Pte ROFT; 25706 Pte HORSE, 57651 Pte HACKSON. I Section No.24th MG Coy attached at 6.25pm. 2 Sections 9th Bn R. Ind. Ches. M.G Coys attacked. Guns lines in def. line Co.	
	24/11		Prepared against enemy attack on BOURLON.	
	25/11/17	1:30am	No.120 MGCoy carried up K.G.K.651 to 121 Coy. Guns useful between GRAINCOURT & SUGAR FACTORY.	
		8am	FIRED on ktt. all from enemy coming back to BOURLON village. Guns going in flanks & light lines by Sgt Ouldby. Indirect K and 1 section junked off.	

Army Form C. 2118.

101 / MGY
121 GO MGBa
40 Ja

Rev Nov VI.

WAR DIARY
or
INTELLIGENCE SUMMARY.
(Erase heading not required.)

Instructions regarding War Diaries and Intelligence Summaries are contained in F. S. Regs., Part II, and the Staff Manual respectively. Title pages will be prepared in manuscript.

Place	Date	Hour	Summary of Events and Information	Remarks and references to Appendices
GRAINCOURT	25.11.17	4 pm	Relieved in the line by 125 M.G. Coy. Company Ndq between Biefvillers & BERTINCOURT and GRAINCOURT. (B)	
	26.11.17	4 am	Company in HINDENBURG SUPPORT LINE. Moved back to BERTINCOURT 9am. Arrived BERTINCOURT 4.50 pm. (B)	
BERTINCOURT	27.11.17	3 am	Marched to YPRES station and entrained for BEAUMETZ where Company arrived at 11 am. Marched thence to billets in REALA CAMP. (Richebourg) W/Para 22)	
BEAUMETZ	28.11.17		Company rested. Roll call. Men showered & witnessed pay.	
	29.11.17		Company continued cleaning all equipment and stores LEHVEKUK 8½ Kts. Pc. Webb etc. Returned from hospital. No.249 #11 249750 Pte O Sk (ananame) returned from Base. No.249012 Pte Grazier J. S.D.	
	30.11.17		Company employed on P.T. heading bow cow arm drill and saluting. (B)	

Vol 19

Confidential

War Diary
- of -
121st Company Machine Gun Corps.
From 1st December 1917 To 31st December 1917

Volume 18.

Army Form C. 2118.

WAR DIARY
or
INTELLIGENCE SUMMARY.
(Erase heading not required.)

Instructions regarding War Diaries and Intelligence Summaries are contained in F. S. Regs., Part II. and the Staff Manual respectively. Title pages will be prepared in manuscript.

Place	Date	Hour	Summary of Events and Information	Remarks and references to Appendices
BELLACOURT	1917 Dec 1st	—	121 M.G. Coy marched from BELLACOURT to ERVILLERS arriving at 6 p.m. 9 later moved back to FERMOY CAMP from 48th M.G. Coy. Weather changeable with rain during early	
ERVILLERS	" 2nd		40 O.R. Reinforcements joined Coy. Coy relieved 49th M.G. Coy in CROISILLES SECTOR. Relief complete by 4 p.m. Enemy quiet during the day. S. CROISILLES shelled during the night. Coy H.Q. established in ST LEGER. Weather - fine	
CROISILLES SECTOR	" 3rd		Enemy quiet. O.C. Coy reconnoitred the line. Weather frosty.	
"	" 4th		Everything very quiet. O.C. Coy reconnoitred the line with a view to reorganising the defence of its Sector. Weather frosty.	
"	" 5		Everything quiet. O.C. Coy reconnoitred line with G.O.C. 121st Bde. 4 guns fired during the night to assist a raid by the Fusiliers on our right.	
"	"		Nine Reinforcements for 4 June joined. Detailed to work on Trm commenced. 2nd LIEUT. AMOS C.E. & 2nd LIEUT. DEACON R.V. joined the Coy from the Base.	

A6945 Wt. W11422/M1160 350,000 12/16 D.D. & L. Forms/C/2118/14.

Army Form C. 2118.

WAR DIARY
or
INTELLIGENCE SUMMARY.

(Erase heading not required.)

Instructions regarding War Diaries and Intelligence Summaries are contained in F. S. Regs., Part II. and the Staff Manual respectively. Title pages will be prepared in manuscript.

Place	Date	Hour	Summary of Events and Information	Remarks and references to Appendices
CROISILLES SECTOR	1917 Dec 6th	-	Enemy quiet. Our artillery active during the day. Major Jones carried out work on gun positions in the line as usual.	
"	Dec 7th	-	2 Lieut WESTWOOD W.I. & 2 Lieut BAKER F.C. joined Coy from the Base. Enemy quiet. O.C. Coy visited the line accompanied by the Divisional Machine Gun Officer.	
"	Dec 8th	-	LIEUT HERBERT proceeded on leave to U.K. Enemy quiet. Work in the line progressing.	
"	Dec 9th	.		
"	Dec 10th	-	Coy relieved by 120th M.G. Coy in CROISILLES SECTOR. Coy proceeded to ERVILLERS & billets were found in ERVILLERS at 6 pm. Orders received as return to the line.	

A6945   Wt. W14422/M1160   350,000   12/16   D. D. & L.   Forms/C./2118/14.

Army Form C. 2118.

WAR DIARY
or
INTELLIGENCE SUMMARY.
(Erase heading not required.)

Instructions regarding War Diaries and Intelligence Summaries are contained in F. S. Regs., Part II. and the Staff Manual respectively. Title pages will be prepared in manuscript.

Place	Date	Hour	Summary of Events and Information	Remarks and references to Appendices
ERVILLERS	1917 Dec 11th	—	Bn moved into position in the ERVILLERS SECTOR, leaving ERVILLERS at 2 a.m. Enemy expected to attack everything in readiness	
CROISELLES	Dec 12th	—	Line heavily shelled by the enemy. Enemy made attack on line EAST of BULLECOURT 15 miles SOUTH. Found heavily shelled.	
"	Dec 13th	—	Enemy still expected to attack. 2 LIEUT THORPE, T. admitted to hospital sick. Enemy artillery active. Heavy shelling in parts of the line. Raid made by Brigade on our right.	
"	Dec 14th	—	Enemy artillery active. Enemy attack did not develop. 2 O.R. seriously wounded. Transport moved from ERVILLERS to MOYENNEVILLE	
"	Dec 15th	—		
"	Dec 16th	—	Enemy fairly quiet. M. Guns fired on hostile movement by day.	

A6945 Wt. W14422/M1160 350,000 12/16 D. D. & L. Forms/C/2118/14.

Army Form C. 2118.

WAR DIARY
or
INTELLIGENCE SUMMARY.
(Erase heading not required.)

Instructions regarding War Diaries and Intelligence Summaries are contained in F. S. Regs., Part II. and the Staff Manual respectively. Title pages will be prepared in manuscript.

Place	Date	Hour	Summary of Events and Information	Remarks and references to Appendices
CROISILLES	1917 Dec 17	—	Enemy fairly quiet	
"	18	—	N.C.O. sniper shot the movement by day. Enemy front covered out. Coy evacuated position occupied & took over position held by 120 Inf. Bg. Lieut THORPE evacuated to U.K. sick	
"	19	—	Enemy quiet	
"	20	—	Night front covered our Enemy artillery inactive	
"	21	—	ST LEGER heavily shelled during the day of harassing. Enemy quiet. Notable activity partly in CEYLON TRENCH dispersed by M.G. fire during the night	
"	22	—	Enemy quiet. 10" enemy mortaring in the areas fired on, no information being received from the infantry — were dispersed. Enemy quiet	
"	23	—	Lieut S.A. WANN proceeded on leave to U.K. 2/Lt NERBERT returned from leave to U.K.	

A6945 Wt. W1422/M1160 350,000 12/16 D.D. & L. Forms/C. 2118/14.

Army Form C. 2118.

WAR DIARY
or
INTELLIGENCE SUMMARY.
(Erase heading not required.)

Instructions regarding War Diaries and Intelligence Summaries are contained in F.S. Regs., Part II and the Staff Manual respectively. Title pages will be prepared in manuscript.

Place	Date	Hour	Summary of Events and Information	Remarks and references to Appendices
CRUISILLES SECTOR	1917 Dec 24th	—	121st M.G. Coy relieved by 120 M.G. Coy. 121st M.G. Coy occupied huts in MOYNE CAMP which were vacated by 120 M.G. Coy	
MOYENNEVILLE	Dec 25th	—	Men attend church parade. O.C. Coy reconnoitred BULLECOURT SECTOR.	
"	Dec 26th	—	Morning spent preparing for the line. Coy moved into line & relieved 76th M.G. Coy in BULLECOURT SECTOR. Relief complete 9.30 p.m. same order to orders of the 76th Infantry Bde.	
BULLECOURT	Dec 27th	—	Enemy Artillery action. O.C. Coy reconnoitred the line. 121st Infantry Bde relieved 76th Infantry Bde. Hostile aircraft flying low was fired on by our machine guns. Artillery on both sides active. Aerial activity on both sides. Hostile aeroplane fired on by our machine guns. Machine guns fired in hostile movement during the day & his now	

LIEUT. FLOOD R.R. joined Coy from the Base.
HAMELINCOURT.

A6945 Wt. W11432/M1160 350,000 12/16 D.D. & L. Forms/C.2118/14

Army Form C. 2118.

WAR DIARY
or
INTELLIGENCE SUMMARY.
(Erase heading not required.)

Instructions regarding War Diaries and Intelligence Summaries are contained in F. S. Regs., Part II. and the Staff Manual respectively. Title pages will be prepared in manuscript.

Place	Date	Hour	Summary of Events and Information	Remarks and references to Appendices
BOUSSCOURT	1917 Dec 29th	—	Enemy artillery active.	
			G.O.C. assumes 12.1st Infantry Battalion aided Machine gun positions in the line accompanied by O.C. Coy.	
			Aircraft Annex of 15 allotted in by Machine guns.	
			Transport Limber moved to ERVILLERS. Enemy Quiet.	
	Dec 30th	—	O.C. Coy reconnoitred line & selected new Gun positions with a view to reoccupying the defence of the line.	
			Two guns fired during the evening in co-operation with Artillery.	
	Dec 31	—	Enemy artillery active along the front of Divison. Coy HQ shelled with gas shells during the early morning.	
			LIEUT HERBERT proceeded to CAMIERS to attend M.G. Demonstration.	

Confidential.

War Diary
—of—
121st Company Machine Gun Corps

From 1st January 1918. To 31st January 1918.

Volume 19.

WAR DIARY or INTELLIGENCE SUMMARY.

Army Form C. 2118.

(Erase heading not required.)

Instructions regarding War Diaries and Intelligence Summaries are contained in F. S. Regs., Part II. and the Staff Manual respectively. Title pages will be prepared in manuscript.

Place	Date	Hour	Summary of Events and Information	Remarks and references to Appendices
BULLECOURT	1918 Jan 1st	—	Enemy quiet during the day	
			Hostile movement sniped by machine gun	
			Work in progress	
"	Jan 2nd	—	Hostile movement sniped by machine guns during the day	
			Night firing carried out in co-operation with the artillery	
			Aerial activity on both sides.	
"	Jan 3rd	—	Enemy artillery active	
			Enemy party found in enemy trench after dispersed. Night firing carried out	
			Lieut. E.G.HERBERT returns from M.G. Barracks Demonstration at CAMIERS.	
"	Jan 4th	—	O.C. visited the line & shook hands with men & inspected positions	
			CAPT. S.G. DAVEY proceeded on leave to U.K. and E.G. HERBERT accompanied	
			command of the company. Major Finn sanctioned.	
"	Jan 5th	—	Enemy attacked our lines & caused a hostile barrage & sent EAST of	
			BULLECOURT Machine gun fired 46,500 rounds on S.O.S. target	
"	Jan 6th	—	Enemy movement sniped during the day. Enemy driven from out previously	
			occupied by us. Enemy M.G. fired during the attack. Enemy gun occupied saphead.	

Army Form C. 2118.

WAR DIARY
or
INTELLIGENCE SUMMARY.
(Erase heading not required.)

Instructions regarding War Diaries and Intelligence Summaries are contained in F. S. Regs., Part II. and the Staff Manual respectively. Title pages will be prepared in manuscript.

Place	Date	Hour	Summary of Events and Information	Remarks and references to Appendices
	1918			
BULLECOURT	Jan 7th	—	Enemy quiet during the day. Enemy shrieves from Sap during the evening. Machine Gun fired during 15' attack.	
			120th M.G.Coy relieved by 233rd M.G.Coy in the line. 6 guns of 120th M.G.Coy relieved 6 of 233rd Coy in the Intermediate line. Remainder of 121st M.G.Coy occupied huts in	
FERNDY CAMP, ERVILLERS.				
ERVILLERS	Jan 8th	—	Day spent in cleaning up. Enemy attacked outpost but gained no footing. 6 guns in the line fired on the S.O.S. signal.	
"	Jan 9th	—	Day spent in training & bathing the men.	
"	Jan 10th	—	Day spent in cleaning & repairing the huts & camp. O.C. by visited the guns in the line.	
"	Jan 11th	—	O.C.Coy reconnoitred Battalion's line with the D.M.G.O. Day spent in training. 6 gun teams from ERVILLERS relieved the 6 teams in the line.	
"	Jan 12th	.	Day spent in training & improving the camp.	

Army Form C. 2118.

WAR DIARY
or
INTELLIGENCE SUMMARY.
(Erase heading not required.)

Instructions regarding War Diaries and Intelligence Summaries are contained in F. S. Regs., Part II. and the Staff Manual respectively. Title pages will be prepared in manuscript.

Place	Date	Hour	Summary of Events and Information	Remarks and references to Appendices
ERVILLERS	1918 Jan 13th	—	Day spent in Ervillers.	
"	Jan 14th	—	O.C. Coy carried out intermediate recce. Work started on Lewis gun position. Enemy quiet.	
"	Jan 15th	—	121st M.G. Coy relieved 223rd Coy M.G.C. in Ervillers Sector. Guns & equipment exchanged. On getting the guns into position among the dead state of the trenches. Two new positions in the Jabinesdale line finished & camouflaged. Lieut S.A. WANN to hospital.	
BULLECOURT	Jan 16th	—	Enemy quiet. Trenches in a bad condition. Work commenced at all gun positions on E.Y. Emplacements & making dugouts & shelters watertight.	
"	Jan 17th	—	Wet weather makes this work arduous. Enemy artillery active. Work on emplacements still continued.	
"	Jan 18th	—	Enemy very quiet. Very little activity in the air. Gun teams work hard to get trenches & vicinity of gun emplacements clear.	

WAR DIARY
or
INTELLIGENCE SUMMARY.

(Erase heading not required.)

Army Form C. 2118.

Place	Date	Hour	Summary of Events and Information	Remarks and references to Appendices
BULECOURT	1918			
	Jan 19th	—	Weather improves. Men working hard repairing emplacements & clearing out trenches.	
	Jan 20th	—	Enemy quiet.	
			Enemy quiet.	
			Capt S. G. DAVEY returned from leave to U.K.	
	Jan 21st	—	Re-netting of trenches in the vicinity of gun positions almost completed.	
			Enemy quiet.	
			Work on site of the Reserve Gun position of No 1 section commenced	
	Jan 22nd	—	Enemy artillery engaged in counter battery work. Working party sent up to assist R.E. at new battery position for No 5 section. STANHOPE REDOUBT. Weather raining.	
	Jan 23rd	—	Enemy artillery active E COAST shelled with gas shells. Lieut R.R. FLOOD proceeded to U.K. on leave.	

Army Form C. 2118.

WAR DIARY
or
INTELLIGENCE SUMMARY.
(Erase heading not required.)

Instructions regarding War Diaries and Intelligence Summaries are contained in F. S. Regs., Part II. and the Staff Manual respectively. Title pages will be prepared in manuscript.

Place	Date	Hour	Summary of Events and Information	Remarks and references to Appendices
BULLECOURT	1917 Jan 24		Enemy quiet.	
			DM.G.O. & G.S.O.1 Division arranged Intermediate Line with O.C. Coy to select new battery position for M.G.	
			Great aerial activity during the fine weather.	
	Jan 25		Hostile aircraft active & O.P's fired on by M.G's.	
			Work in the progress. Wire connected to new "E" Battery position in Intermediate Line.	
	Jan 26		2 Lieut ELLIS proceeded to LE HAMEAU on an anti-aircraft course with R.F.C.	
			Enemy quiet — weather frosty.	
			2nd Lieut S.R. WANN struck off strength of Coy.	
			Wire in and battery positions progressing.	
	Jan 27		Weather still frosty.	
			D.M.G.O. visited him with O.C. Coy to inspect new "B" Battery M.G. position.	
			Hostile artillery active during the night.	
			Hostile aircraft bombed areas behind our line during evening.	

WAR DIARY
or
INTELLIGENCE SUMMARY.
(Erase heading not required.)

Army Form C. 2118.

Place	Date	Hour	Summary of Events and Information	Remarks and references to Appendices
BULLECOURT	1918 Jan 26th	—	Artillery active. Both sides. Shell burst "Blue"	
			Lieut. J. G. DUNCAN joined Coy from the Base.	
			Gun positions 28d.7.0.6., 9.9.99 occupied with "A" Bat'y	
			position. 3rd Lieut F. ELLIS reports the Coy from RFC and D'aerial 1st eleven are	
			Hostile aircraft active towards wood picked up	
			No. Sergt MONTGOMERY wounded	
	Jan 27	—	Heavy artillery on both sides. Enemy planes bombed back areas during the night	
			During evening enemy raid during to depth of 50	
			hostile m.g. active during the night.	
			Difficulty about drinking water supply with Sig shells & H.E.	
			Have the mountain battery to the far down the day.	
	Jan 28		Night very quiet	
			Hostile longe range fire in our neighbourhood in G	
			Tried enfilade with longrange M.G. attacks on	
					the enemy	

Army Form C. 2118.

WAR DIARY
or
INTELLIGENCE SUMMARY.
(Erase heading not required.)

Place	Date	Hour	Summary of Events and Information	Remarks and references to Appendices
BULLECOURT	1918 Jan 31st	—	Enemy very quiet. Sniping by m.g. reportedly owing to our f.o.s. Night firing carried out on hostile tracks.	

S. Dewsy OC
1/21 M.G. Bn

CONFIDENTIAL.

WAR DIARY.

OF

"C" Coy. 40th Div. M.G. Battalion.

FROM 1st February 1918 TO 28th February 1918.

(VOLUME 20)

1-21 MGC

Army Form C. 2118.

WAR DIARY
or
INTELLIGENCE SUMMARY.
(Erase heading not required.)

Instructions regarding War Diaries and Intelligence Summaries are contained in F. S. Regs., Part II. and the Staff Manual respectively. Title pages will be prepared in manuscript.

Place	Date	Hour	Summary of Events and Information	Remarks and references to Appendices
BULLECOURT.	1918 Feb 1st	—	Artillery activity in both sides. T.O.s interfere with snipers by day. Nights fairly carried out. R.E. assistance obtained to make new emplacements for "A" Battery M.G. position. All guns laid on their new S.O.S. lines in co-operation with the machine gun Coys in right & left Bn.	
"	Feb 2nd		Hostile movement fired on by M.G. by day. 2 hits obtained. Enemy firing carried out. Work on line continued.	
"	Feb 3rd		Hostile movement fired on by M.G. during the day. 3 hits obtained. Enemy firing carried out in co-operation with the artillery.	
"	Feb 4th		Hostile movement fired on by machine guns during the day, 5 hits obtained. Work in the line progressing.	
"	Feb 5th		Artillery active on both sides. Hostile movement fired on. 3 hits obtained. Work in the line progressing.	

Army Form C. 2118.

WAR DIARY
or
INTELLIGENCE SUMMARY.
(Erase heading not required.)

Instructions regarding War Diaries and Intelligence Summaries are contained in F. S. Regs., Part II. and the Staff Manual respectively. Title pages will be prepared in manuscript.

Place	Date	Hour	Summary of Events and Information	Remarks and references to Appendices
BULLECOURT	1918. Feb 6th	—	Artillery on both sides active during the night. Less movement than by day during the day. 2 hits obtained. Night firing carried out in co-operation with the artillery. Work on new M.G. positions continues.	
"	Feb 7th	—	Artillery activity during the day. Hostile movement sniped by M.G. Was now commanded Lt. Dunnison of M.G. Battalion visited Coy H.Q. COLONEL ROBERT	
"	Feb 8th	—	S.O.S. signal sent up at 6.30 a.m. in our front in the front of the Left Brigade. 33,500 rounds fired by machine guns on S.O.S. lines. Heavy hostile barrage put down in the weak gun casualties nil. M.G. fired during the night in co-operation with the artillery in areas in which a good deal of movement was seen by day.	
"	Feb 9th	—	M.G. fired at 3.45 a.m. in co-operation with artillery. Artillery observers reported extremely satisfactory results. Lieut R R FLOOD returned from leave to U.K. 1 Officer and 17 M.G. Coy attached to Coy for two days. Hostile movement fired on during the day by machine guns. Night firing carried out in co-operation with the artillery.	

WAR DIARY or INTELLIGENCE SUMMARY

Army Form C. 2118.

Place	Date	Hour	Summary of Events and Information	Remarks and references to Appendices
BULLECOURT	1918 Feb 10	-	Weather inclement. Snowfall during m.S's during the day. Rifles fines carried out in preparation with the artillery. Work in progress.	
	Feb 11	-	Weather inclement. Rifles during the morning C. Night firing carried out. 1 Officer & 10 O.R's 177 M.G.Coy returned to their unit. Enemy artillery active during the night.	
"	Feb 12	-	Enemy very quiet. 12:00 m.S.Coy relieved by 177 M.G.Coy in the BULLECOURT Sector. 12:30 m.S.Coy proceeded by march to MOYNIE CAMP MOYENNEVILLE	
MOYENNEVILLE	Feb 13	-	Day spent in cleaning guns, gun equipment, repairing linkers etc.	
"	Feb 14	-	Moving about in preparing to move. Coy paraded at 11:15 a.m & marched to No.4 Camp HENDECOURT.	
No.4 Camp	Feb 15	-	Company cleaning guns equipment and limbers. Not leaving HENDECOURT until noon. Cleaning/camp/ Company refitteds men's clothes & necessaries.	
HENDECOURT	Feb 16		Company morning correcting of P.T. Squad drill Throwshots. Cleaning ?	

A584 Wt W4973/M687 750,000 8/16 D.D.&L. Ltd Form C.2118/13

Army Form C. 2118.

WAR DIARY
or
INTELLIGENCE SUMMARY.
(Erase heading not required.)

Instructions regarding War Diaries and Intelligence Summaries are contained in F.S. Regs., Part II. and the Staff Manual respectively. Title pages will be prepared in manuscript.

Place	Date	Hour	Summary of Events and Information	Remarks and references to Appendices
N.4 CAMP HENDECOURT	22.11.17		O.C. Coy and Section Officers reconnoitred + Battery Positions in Reserve Area around HENIN and BECQUEREL, in case of Enemy break through. The Company were detailed Hostile Air Raid in neighbouring District occurred 10 p.m. midnight, + a gas mounted (manned until all clear" signal was given. Coy cleaning + bundling	
	18		Battalion Parade at 8.30 A.M. C.O. inspected boys present. C.O. inspected Transport Limbers at 11 A.M. Battalion training commenced 15-day Tactical + Technical Course for all Officers, specl. Orderly Officers was started. Major R.G.V. ROBERTS M.C. and Capt. S.G. DAVEY in charge. Battalion training consisted of Squad Drill, Musketry, Immediate action, Physical Training, Bayonet fighting and Stripping guns, Aim Alarm given at 7 pm. + Guns were quickly manned	
DURHAM CAMP BOISLEUX AU MONT.	19.		Coy left Hut Camp Hendecourt at 10 AM. and succeeded to DURHAM CAMP Boisleux au Mont. Campl Thoroughly cleaned before departure and on arrival at New Camp.	
	20		C.O. went to Courcelt Baume Point Coy went while 1 Bn Coy at ERVILLERS. Continuing training + taking fixing at Camp. Casablanca, Sydney Room etc.	
	21		Company training. OC Coy lectured Officers on the Podium Orders from DHQ received AM11P.M.K mounted in Reserve as HENIN BECQUEREL ST MARTIN see 16 guns in action 1.7-15 pm. Trial.	
	22		Compy training. OC lectured Officers on Barrage work such precaution in the afternoon 16.30 Coy K Lecture Officer Res.	
	23		Company training Shapes. OC Coy lectured Officers on Precaution and NCOs in attack.	

A5834 Wt.W4973/M687 750,000 8/16 D.D. & L. Ltd. Forms/C.1112/13.

Army Form C. 2118.

WAR DIARY
or
INTELLIGENCE SUMMARY.
(Erase heading not required.)

Instructions regarding War Diaries and Intelligence Summaries are contained in F. S. Regs., Part II. and the Staff Manual respectively. Title pages will be prepared in manuscript.

Place	Date	Hour	Summary of Events and Information	Remarks and references to Appendices
DURHAM CAMP BOISLEUX AU MONT	July 1/17		Company on Church Parade & attigned Conference of Coy Commanders at BERNEVILLERS re new organisation of Battalion.	
	2		G.O. Brownsfield Company life (apx 3)	
	3		Company training under Coy and Section Officers. Recce'd Reserve Postions B20 - B26 with a view to taking over from	
			during Coy	
BORROW GUT MARL	27		Company practised approach of Mar 9.15 AM antering ah DURROWS 11.40 AM Trunsport at Sucteme Coombey. leaving Dublin Redoubt on the other side of Coy on arriving sent three Coys as Lieut Batn left in charge of Courbard. On being unable see's of 21st G. 50th Division sent to Mancing BC & down into "B" Positions not serving into during Party at might which moved forward towards BRAY during morning of 28 & all reconnaissances sent to 50 Div SS.	

R.H.Clay Lt Col
O.C. 19 Battalion